HOW TO EAT LIKE AN ASSHOLE

observations about food, nutrition, and manners by the Juice Nazi

Andrew An Ho

Foodyap

Copyright © 2020 Andrew An Ho

All rights reserved

The characters and events portrayed in this book are fictitious. Any similarity to real persons, living or dead, is coincidental and not intended by the author.

No part of this book may be reproduced, or stored in a retrieval system, or transmitted in any form or by any means, electronic, mechanical, photocopying, recording, or otherwise, without express written permission of the publisher.

ISBN-13: 9798632709248
ISBN-10: 1477123456

Cover design by: Art Painter
Library of Congress Control Number: 2018675309
Printed in the United States of America

This book is dedicated to my customers. You've put up with so much from me and still support me. Hugs and kisses.

The simple is carefully shunned by those who labour to seem what they would be.

PAUL FUSSELL

CONTENTS

Title Page

Copyright

Dedication

Epigraph

Chapter 1 How to Eat Like an Asshole — 4

Chapter 2 Redneck Food is Healthier Than Stupid Middle-Class American Food — 14

Chapter 3 Stop Buying This Shit (if you want to save money) — 22

Chapter 4 Why We Don't Carry Wheatgrass — 27

Chapter 5 How to Eat with Instincts — 38

Chapter 6 How to Order the Nasty Shit — 44

Chapter 7 Why We Eat What We Eat — 47

Chapter 8 Why People Prefer Bad Service — 62

Chapter 9 Why Being Nice Will Kill You — 73

Chapter 10 The Alive Juice Bar Diet — 77

Chapter 11 Why People Hate McDonald's — 82

Chapter 12 Soy, Men, and Titties — 93

Chapter 13 How to Get Kids To Eat Their Veggies and To Love Their Parents — 101

Chapter 14 Do You Have Feelings About Feelings? — 115

Chapter 15 How the Cult of Self-Esteem Produces Fuck Ups	128
Chapter 16 What the Story of Echo and Narcissus Tells Us About Self-Love	139
Chapter 17 Why People Don't Change	143
About The Author	152
Praise For Author	154
Books In This Series	160
Books By This Author	164

ANDREW AN AN HO

Introduction

I work at a juice bar. Juice bars are unlike conventional restaurants because their purpose isn't solely to entertain the customer, but also to guide them about health and diet matters. I don't just cook nutritious drinks and meals that taste good to the customer (taste comes first, taste always comes first), I'm expected to nurse sick customers back to health, to prescribe remedies to heal an injury, and to absolve those who've committed dietary debauchery. That's a lot of conflicting roles and needs to balance — I have to be stern and funny, candid and soothing, and my food has to be salubrious yet pleasurable.

My (sometimes clumsy) attempts at balance to make sense of the absurdities of American life is the driving theme throughout the 17 essays in this book. In the eponymous opening chapter, I show how what's commonly considered as Anglo-American good table manners is actually bullying masquerading as good breeding that makes eating a tortuous rather than pleasurable experience. Chapter 2, *Redneck Food is Healthier Than Stupid Middle Class Food*, takes aim at stereotypes about Rednecks and redneck cuisine and posits that it's actually the diet and sensibilities of the American middle-class that's fucked up. We segue into chapter 3, *Stop Buying This Shit*, for more detailed examples of stupid, expensive shit people buy in their attempts to live healthier lives.

In chapter 4, *Why We Don't Carry Wheatgrass*, the essay in this book I'm most proud of, we move on to supplements of dubious value. This chapter begins with a take-down of Wheatgrass as a tonic and then asks what our attraction to snake-oils reveals about human nature. Chapter 5, *How to Eat With Instincts*, is about how and why we've learned to stop eating with instincts and how we can get them back. In chapter 6, *How to Order the Nasty Shit*, you learn how to order the Chinese food Chinese people eat. We pivot, in chapter 7, *Why We Eat What We Eat*, to a history of American cuisine to understand how and why certain ingredients became nasty to most Americans.

My juice bar is known for "bad service." We address this reputation in chapter 8, *Why People Prefer Bad Service*, which turns middle-class American notions of "good service" on its head to reveal an American middle-class culture rife with politeness grandstanding and obsequious bullying. The topsy-turvy questioning of "good manners" continues in chapter 9, *Why Being Nice Will Kill You*. Here I note the correlation between nice personalities (personality type C) and diets high in sugar and processed food. Chapter 10 introduces *The Alive Juice Bar Diet* that's not quite a diet. See, balancing!

Chapter 11 asks *Why People Hate McDonald's* and I guarantee you it's not what you think, this will surprise the fuck out of you. Chapter 12, *Soy, Men, and Titties*, tackles rumors that about soy messing with people's estrogen levels, making men grow titties. Chapter 13 is about *How to Get Kids to Eat Their Veggies and to Love Their Parents* because most of them are doing neither.

The final four chapters are about why people are fucked in the head. We begin with *Do You Have Feelings about Feelings*, in chapter 14 to figure out why Americans are some of the most emotionally repressed and broken people in the history of the world. Chapter 15, *How the Cult of Self-Esteem Produces Fuck Ups*, looks at the consequences of the self-esteem movement and how self-esteem is wrongly confused with self-confidence and the correlation between the two is actually inverted. Chapter 16, *What the Story of Echo and Narcissus Tells Us About Self-Love*, is a moralistic re-reading of a tragedy. Chapter 17, *Why People Don't Change*, is about why it's so hard to get people to change their diets and other habits.

Though the essays are intentionally ordered and grouped, they can be read independently from each other. Enjoy and comments are appreciated and can be sent to Foodyap@gmail.com.

More books coming soon, including "How to Cook Like a Racist," where we offer cooking tips and lessons in the context of American racial politics.

CHAPTER 1 HOW TO EAT LIKE AN ASSHOLE

British etiquette expert William Hanson teaches people to eat like assholes.

This asshole eats with a chopstick up his ass.

Here's an excerpt of him teaching etiquette on British TV show *Let's Do Lunch With Gino and Mel,* Gino (who is Italian) as Hanson's foil:

Asshole: *No...this is how we eat peas.*

Gino: *First of all, the spoon is much easier because it goes in the spoon easily and you can shovel it in your mouth.*

Asshole: No, we use a fork. Like this. Then we push the peas, with the back of our knife, onto the fork like this and eat it like this. The tines of the fork should always be facing down. (Fork turned down).

Gino: So by the time you finish the peas, my steak will be cold, my mashed potatoes will be freezing cold, if we do it one by one the way you do it.

Gino has a point, Anglo dining etiquette is inefficient, it makes eating a lot more difficult than necessary. What's the point of etiquette then? From Wiki:

Etiquette is the set of conventional rules of personal behaviour in polite society, usually in the form of an ethical code that delineates the expected and accepted social behaviors that accord with the conventions and norms observed by a society, a social class, or a social group.

So the point of Anglo dining etiquette is to teach people to look down on those who prefer to not make dining out a tortuous experience. In other words, it teaches people to act like assholes, bullies really. But it doesn't have to be like that, here's my counterpoint definition of etiquette:

Good etiquette: rules of conduct to maximize ease and efficiency and to keep costs down while benefiting the greater good.

Bad etiquette: rules of conduct that allows one to covertly spotlight one's narcissistic needs (eg. recognition as the world's nicest and classiest person) at the expense of the greater good.

Which is the purpose of etiquette in most non-Anglo cultures, it's a way to lubricate social interactions instead of complicating them. How complicated? Check this shit out.

How to Eat Soup Like an Asshole

Summary of steps:

1. Position your body two hand widths away from the table
2. Use correct spoon, the one with the largest bowl
3. Spoon soup at and toward the twelve o'clock side of the bowl using the outer edge of spoon. (Am I losing you)?
4. Gently scrape off soup that's on the bottom of the spoon along the twelve o'clock edge of the bowl.
5. Bring the edge of the spoon that faces you to mouth without spilling or hunching over.
6. Sip soup without making noise
7. Repeat process, inserting a chopstick up the ass each time.

Got it? Didn't think so. And that's a good thing, only fucktards think it's ok to serve and eat soup this way. To begin with, what's with the shallow bowl and the plate it's on? Sure, it looks kinda pretty, but so does Paris Hilton's pussy, doesn't mean you should serve sushi on it.

ANDREW AN AN HO

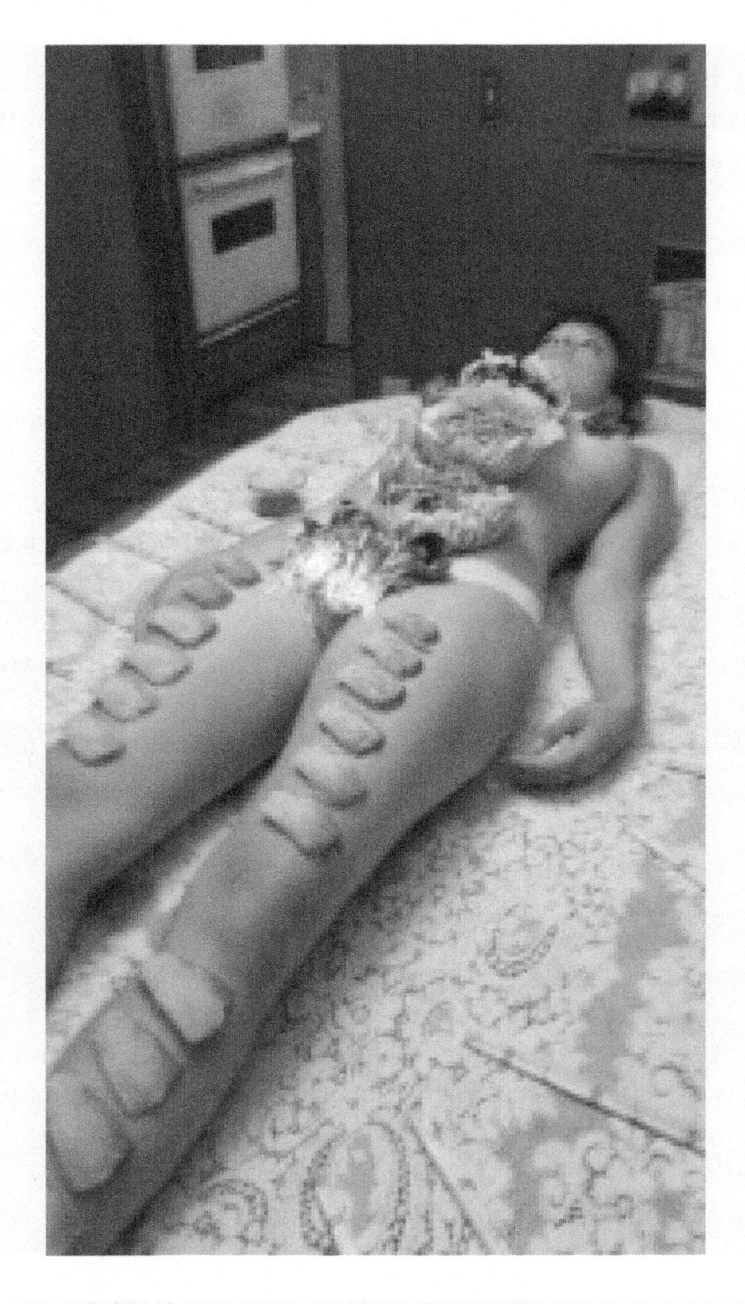

Nyotaimori dinners are pretty to look at, ridiculous to serve.

And as Gino points out, how long is eating it this way going to

HOW TO EAT LIKE AN ASSHOLE

take? What happens to the integrity of the soup if it takes someone 10 excruciating minutes to finish it? The good news is that there are a few American chefs who reject tormenting their customers that way by instead putting soup in a teacup from which they drink, no spoon involved.

It's ok to stare at Paris Hilston's STD ridden snatch that needs a shave. Bad idea to eat off of it.

How to Eat Miso Soup and Ramen Properly

Here's how the Japanese eat miso soup: no spoon, chopsticks only. Some of you are like, WTF? No, fuck you, you're the weird one.

8

*This is how miso soup is served in Japan. NO SPOON!
And never a stupid shallow bowl.*

How to eat miso soup Japanese way:

1. With one hand, bring bowl of soup to your mouth. Start drinking.
2. Use chopsticks on the other hand to pick out floating pieces of food.
3. Repeat process

That's it, it's easy as fuck as long as you know how to use chopsticks. But it feels unnatural to most Americans because they've been trained to think of drinking from a bowl as vulgar. Well how the fuck so? Because some asshole said so?

Here's a video on how to eat ramen, a dish Americans love but look awkward — like some fat guy trying ballet for the first time — while eating.

Summary:

1. You can use chopsticks only or use chopsticks to put food on a big spoon and eat from a spoon. (I prefer the latter method to prevent hunching, which is bad for you).

2. You can slurp if you want. (He does).
3. "Ramen is an open format, you can eat it any way you want to."
4. "But one thing I want to emphasize is that you shouldn't take too much time to eat this because the noodles will expand...it shouldn't take more than five minutes for you to finish."

This chef eats with chopsticks instead of shoving them up his ass. The only hard rule involves the integrity of the food: finish within five minutes or you're ruining the food that someone worked hard on for you to enjoy. How you finish your ramen is up to you, and that includes drinking from the bowl.

Contrast this approach to food to the asshole way of dining. Which is more fun, which makes food taste better? Which turns eating into a cumbersome social competition? Do you prefer to enjoy your food, or would you prefer to show off your fake good breeding while eating?

How to Eat Soup

Sometimes I fuck with customers. Let's say I'm making ham soup and purposely cut the ham too big to fit on the spoon. Then I watch, do they struggle through using a spoon, or do they switch to a fork to eat the ham and drink the broth from the cup, which is the sensible act to do?

So how should we eat soup without looking like assholes? Serve and eat it in any way you want, not how others want you to eat. Which is going to be tough if you care about what others think of you. (In which case you have serious problems). At any rate, that's all there is to it, once you block out etiquette, your instincts will tell you how something should be eaten.

How to Eat Chinese Style (chopstick hack)

Southern Chinese food is typically served with a bowl of rice and an assortment of dishes. This creates an awkward situation for many gweilos (foreign devils), especially if they want the cultural experience of using chopsticks. Here's what you're supposed to do: use one hand to bring bowl of rice off the table, use chopsticks to grab whatever you want to put on rice. Bring the bowl close to your mouth, use chopsticks to put whatever you want into mouth. So the space between grabbing something with chopsticks to bringing it to mouth is shortened, making it less likely that you'll drop what you grabbed and become frustrated. If you want to get really Chinese, bring the bowl to your mouth and use chopsticks to shovel food in your mouth. Make as much noise as you want. It's actually very easy, very natural to eat that way, far easier than using a knife and fork. It's jarring to watch people switch knife and fork from one hand to another for the sake of propriety. (Stop switching)! In fact, this American fork and knife switcheroo habit was picked up from pretentious 19th century Europeans who later on decided that it is in fact pretentious and tortuous, so they stopped doing it. But Americans didn't get the message that it was no longer in vogue in Europe.

Pet peeve: Chinese restaurants that serve food on plate and then give you chopsticks to eat with. That's a mismatch of cultural habits. In this case, a knife and fork and spoon make more sense. Chopsticks work best when the food is served Chinese style, not on plates, which in Chinese dining is only used as the place to hold food and discarded bones.

This foreign devil knows how to eat Chinese food. You can eat this way too!

Why We Eat Like Assholes

Because we're fake as fuck. An asshole is someone who makes up bizarre and arbitrary rules of conduct solely to exclude those who won't play along. Play anthropologist and look around: you can probably make sense of why Ethiopians, Chinese, Japanese, Mexicans, Indians, Peruvians, Italians, Rednecks…eat as they do. And then you get to Anglo cultures and see some stuff that makes sense, and then a bunch of stuff that makes no sense. Where assholes tell other assholes to do stupid shit, to act like piece of shits who make ugly shit, fucked up shit, crazy shit, worthless shit, and dodo shit that's somehow perversely considered as elegant and charming by those who look like monkey shit. Where politeness is confused with civility, niceness with kindness, and eating with a chopstick up one's ass with good breeding.

How White Anglo Saxon Pricks at Downton Abbey eat, with chopsticks up their asses.

Compare the above two "How to" videos again, pretend you're an alien studying human behavior this time around. Which culture do you find bizarre, the one with a bunch of precise rules that make it harder to eat, or the one that only has one hard rule — finish ramen within 5 minutes to ensure integrity of noodles — everything else is up to you?

Sane people don't make life harder for themselves. And did you know that the Japanese eat sushi with their hands? Nom nom.

CHAPTER 2 REDNECK FOOD IS HEALTHIER THAN STUPID MIDDLE-CLASS AMERICAN FOOD

Redneck cuisine is better for the environment too. I'll prove it.

Take roadkill cuisine, which according to Wiki is "considered unglamorous and mocked in pop culture, where it is often associated with stereotypes of rednecks and uncouth persons." Below are some of the advantages of roadkill meat:

- low cost
- organic meat that's naturally high in vitamins and proteins with lean meat and little saturated fat
- organic meat that's free of antibiotics and other drugs
- organic meat that doesn't come from animals who lived in filthy overcrowded cages and pens

Meaning those deplorable roadkill scavengers are eating food that's healthier and more environmentally friendly than the over-priced, over-modified, over-hyped and environmentally destructive bullshit people buy at Whole Foods. More examples of how Redneck food is superior later. Let's first take a look at what middle-class America thinks everyone should eat.

Why Middle Class America eats "BAD" food

Because the American middle-class doesn't define itself in terms of economic clout and technological sophistication. This demographic instead defines itself *against* another group, usually Rednecks (and otherwise the One Percent). And that's precisely why the American middle-class — the most medicated demographic in the world — can't think straight as consumers and make ridiculous demands to indulge their delusions about themselves. In this batshit crazy world, decisions are based less on practical considerations and more on identity politics. That's why middle-class Americans have a habit of wanting to eat "BAD" food, as Paul Fussell puts it:

...in fruits and vegetables, "pretty" has overtaken actual, honest, and safe in the Basic American Diet. What he's getting at is the scandal of cosmeticizing produce to make it attractive to the ignorant — coloring oranges orange, for instance, or breeding apples and cherries and strawberries so impressively large that they're quite tasteless. Now, in violation of all natural laws, apples are spotchless, wormless, and lustrously red or green. Grapefruits are perfectly round, as firm as baseballs and as yellow as forsythia, and these phony appearances — BAD in a nutshell — are produced by an infinite number of exotic and untested constituents, residing in the chemicals used to bring on these freaks of visual vegetable perfection.

Middle America isn't satisfied with botoxing and medicating just themselves, they have to botox and medicate their fruits and vegetables too because pompous people need pompous things, including pompous inbred food that looks like this.

Middle-class Americans like their produce the way they like their people – everything should look the same.

instead of fruit and vegetables that may look like this:

and is superior in taste and nutrition to their uniformly "pretty" counterparts. American middle class buy with their eyes instead of their minds, as if shopping for a street whore.

If this bizarre consumer demand for cosmetic uniformity of produce is a reflection of Middle-Class America's intolerance for diversity of thought and personality, then what might the absence of fish and fowl heads on their dinner tables suggest about their psychological state? Fussell again:

This manifestation of BAD does accord with American disinclination to accept unpleasant facts, like the cruel fact that oranges are really greenish-yellow and often ovoid, and the wormless apple is really an anomaly that, without dye and polish, will look pretty shabby.

There's no demographic in history that's this uncomfortable with being uncomfortable. And not just uncomfortable with racy and racist jokes and reminders that what they're eating was once alive, these kooky conformists expect eating to be as easy as sucking on mommy's tits back when they were babies. That's why we have chicken nuggets, because they're boneless and already cut up. That's why there are no fish bones, ever. The American middle-class eat like three year olds, which would be fine if they'd shut up and stop projecting their mommy and daddy issues onto those who just want to be left alone.

How fish is served in most parts of the world: head and fins on, bones inside. Fish bones, brains, cartilage and fat are nutritious, containing extra-high levels of vitamin A, omega-3 fatty acids, iron, zinc and calcium.

Travel around the world and you'll see that people aren't this

HOW TO EAT LIKE AN ASSHOLE

squeamish and pampered when it comes to eating (except among the middle class in Anglo nations such as Canada and UK). This isn't normal, it's not healthy or tasty to eat this way (bones enhance flavor and provide essential nutrients) and it's wasteful to discard edible food.

Roast duck is sold with head and penis on at Chinese butcheries. Notice the unusually large penis on third duck from right.

How Rednecks roast an entire pig, head, penis, and hoofs still on. Recycling old bicycle because Rednecks are innovative and care about the environment.

Examples of "BAD" food

The merely bad, Fussell points out, is "something like dog-do on

18

the sidewalk, or a failing grade." "BAD" taste, on the other hand, is anything "phony, clumsy, witless, untalented, vacant, or boring that many Americans can be persuaded is genuine, graceful, bright, or fascinating." Here are more examples from past and present of BAD food middling America has and does enjoy because they think it's healthier and/or tastier and/or more ethical when it's not:

- Skinless chicken breast (pay more for less!)
- Extra lean ground beef (pay more for less!)
- Kobe beef burgers (asshole burger, pay more for fat that will be cooked off)
- Margarine (Frankenbutter)
- White bread (Frankenbread)
- Acai bowls (want to buy one so I can throw it at someone)
- Fortune cookies (over a billion Chinese have asked: "who comes up with this shit?")
- Processed cheese (Frankencheese)

You can be sure that once middle-class America figures out that what they're eating is actually BAD — like with margarine and white bread — cultural amnesia will set in and they'll accuse Rednecks of perpetrating BAD culture.

HOW TO EAT LIKE AN ASSHOLE

REDNECKS, QUEERS, & COUNTRY MUSIC
NADINE HUBBS

Author is a Redneck Dyke. She says that middle-class Americans, not Rednecks, were the homophobes. Now that it's not fashionable to be homophobic, middle-class America blames Rednecks for perpetrating homophobia when all they want is to not be told what to say and think.

Examples of Redneck food that's good for you

- Pig's trotters (collagen good for skin and joint health)
- Oxtail soup (best bone cut for broth that promotes joint health. Now upscale food)
- Livermush (pig's head and liver molded into pate, a

variation of which I recently had at a high end restaurant)
- Chitterlings (pig intestine contains lots of selenium which reduces risk of heart disease and asthma)
- Squirrel (we're overrun with gray squirrels. Tastes sweet and nutty).

After bobbing for pig's feet competition, this Redneck shows us how he eats his pig feet. Which is similar to how a Mexican eats pig feet.

Aside from the squirrel, the above is what people from most parts of the world eat. If what one eats is a reflection of one's values and character, who do you think is more tolerant and open minded and responsible, the Redneck or the middle class American? Who demands total conformity of manners and taste? Who lacks conviction and lives according to the latest fashion and fads? Who lives in an over-sanitized world maintained by intolerance and fear? Who is the ignorant, uncouth fucktard now?

CHAPTER 3 STOP BUYING THIS SHIT (IF YOU WANT TO SAVE MONEY)

Below is a list of some grocery items people buy that they shouldn't buy if they want to save money and have a healthier diet.

6. Orange juice. Sure, it has Vitamin C. So does bell pepper, broccoli, kale and so on and so forth...WITHOUT the sugar. Most fruits should be eaten — as a smoothie is fine, it still has the fiber — not drunk as a juice.

5. Skinless Chicken Breast

Why pay more for less? First, the skin helps keep the muscle meat moist when you cook it. Second, skin has collagen, which helps your skin look young. Third, skin is flavorful and without it, people are going to drench the chicken in gravy or ranch dressing or something like that. Fourth, if you really don't want to eat skin (which is good for you as long as you don't eat too much of it), take it off yourself. Is it really worth paying more to have someone else take it off for you?

4. Lean ground beef

If the goal is to make a burger, keep in mind that most of the fat will be cooked off anyway. So regardless of how fatty the ground beef is, you end up with the same end product. If it's to make spaghetti or meatloaf, you can drain the fat yourself. Though I *don't recommend wasting any part of an animal* — the fat can, for instance, be used to stir fry veggies or to make a confit — because it isn't animal fat that makes people fat and sick, it's the gargantuan PORTION SIZES and excessive sugar intake that does.

Average Dinner Plate Size

In American Restaurants | In American Homes | In Europe

HealingPowerHour.com

3. Kobe ground beef

Kobe ground beef is known for its high fat content. So why does it cost more than lean ground beef, which in turn costs more than its fattier counterparts? Because we live in the Land of

Confusion, where we're taught to trust strangers with impressive sounding titles and degrees instead of our instincts.

In any case, the fat will be cooked off if you're using it to make a burger, so you're paying a premium for nothing. If you prefer more fat in your spaghetti, the cheapest ground beef available will provide comparable amount of fat at a much lower price.

And the celebrated tenderness of Kobe beef doesn't apply to the ground version, because ground beef, by definition, is already tender.

2. Chicken breast

Dark meat is preferred in most parts of the world because it's much more flavorful and juicier than its white counterpart. But not in the Land of Confusion, where white meat is wrongly considered the healthier option just because White supremacy insists that all things "White," regardless of species, must be superior to anything "Dark," it contains less fat and fewer calories than its dark counterpart. Dark meat offers more zinc, riboflavin, niacin, thiamine, taurine, vitamins B12 and B6, and iron than does White meat.

So quit acting like a fucking racist and eat some dark meat. The only reason why so many people tolerate White people meat is because it's been infused with broth so that it's as juicy as the juiciest, biggest dark meat you've ever had. Or they counter the dryness and lack of flavor by drenching it in gravies and sauces to make it palatable, which significantly increases caloric intake.

So to save money and to eat fewer calories, buy dark meat instead of white meat.

1. Meal Kits

They're expensive — $10-$15/person per meal — and no, they don't teach anyone how to cook anymore than the Kama Sutra teaches people how to have sex (which isn't its purpose anyway). Cooking isn't a matter of following recipes, it's about engaging the senses and releasing the instincts. These meal kits are an extension of an education system that teaches people to follow someone else's procedures instead of figuring out how to do something on one's own. And in any case, there are cheaper ways to learn how to cook with recipes (youtube, recipe books), just as there are cheaper ways to get an education than going to school.

Conclusion

Point is, trust your instincts. Listen to your body, it'll tell you what you need and how much to eat. To do that, you need to block out the noise of marketing scams and confusing proclamations about what is or isn't healthy for you. There'll be a post about how to eat with your instincts soon.

HOW TO EAT LIKE AN ASSHOLE

This meal kit cost $30 and takes most people 40 minutes to prepare. This meal kit is like college: both are rip offs that make people poor and stupid.

CHAPTER 4 WHY WE DON'T CARRY WHEATGRASS

Discussion about why we don't name any ingredient a "super" anything and really really offensive material about Oprah and White people farther down. First, let's get this wheatgrass debate settled.

We don't carry wheatgrass, despite demand for it. Here's why:

From random uncredentialed guy writing on Skeptico blog: **Wheatgrass is for Cows**

Summary: Wheatgrass is for cows, not humans, as humans are unable to digest it as cows do.

But why should we trust some random guy on random blogsite?

From Webmd: **Wheatgrass Claims**

Summary: Review of independent peer reviewed studies of wheatgrass show that there's little or no evidence of its purported health benefits to those who drink it.

But that's just another website, the article isn't peer reviewed, and we don't know if author left out studies in his review. So let's go with a renown Naturopath who is also an MD.

From Dr. Andrew Weil, MD (from Harvard), undergrad in Botany (from Harvard); founder of Arizona Center for Integrative Medicine. Currently Clinical Professor of Medicine, a Professor of Public Health, and the Lovell-Jones Professor of Integrative Rheumatology at University of Arizona School of Medicine: **Wheatgrass Does Not Deliver**

Summary: Wheatgrass is bullshit. Key quotes:

On benefits of chlorophyll*: chlorophyll, the green pigment that gives plants their color, has no nutritional role in the human body, a fact that hasn't stopped promoters from making extravagant claims for it. Secondly, there's no evidence to suggest that wheatgrass or chlorophyll are substitutes for 2.2 pounds of vegetables. If you search the medical literature for "wheatgrass," you find very few entries and none at all suggesting that it has any health benefits for humans.*

Nutritionally speaking, wheatgrass simply doesn't deliver on the promoters' promises. I certainly wouldn't recommend substituting it for any of the fresh vegetables and fruits in your diet. Spend your money on good, organically produced food, not on wheatgrass or other sprouts or grasses marketed as "super-foods."

From American Cancer Society, which has provided funding to 47 Nobel Lauretes: **Review of Wheatgrass**

Summary: No evidence AND beware of supplements generally,

as the actual amount of ingredient consumer wants varies. Person who made wheatgrass a health fad was a quack and batshit crazy.

In 1982, the Massachusetts Attorney General sued Wigmore for claiming that her program could reduce or eliminate the need for insulin in diabetics. She later retracted her claims. In 1988, the Massachusetts Attorney General sued Wigmore again, this time for claiming that an "energy enzyme soup" she invented could cure AIDS. Wigmore was ordered to stop representing herself as a physician or person licensed to treat disease. Although Wigmore died in 1993, her Creative Health Institute is still active. Wheatgrass is readily available, and her diet is still in use.

So what is it about human nature that allows so many people — the highly intelligent included, even Steve Jobs gets duped — to buy snake-oils like wheatgrass, to believe in bullshit?

Human Nature
If there's anything to be learned from Cultural Anthropology (and there's not much), it's that as social structure evolves — feudalism to capitalism, for instance — social codes and archetypes from one era reappear in another in a different form. Example: Aunt Jemima, year 1900. She's loved by White people because she takes good care of them. Mammy, the "house nigger" archetype. Oprah Winfrey, year 2000. Same shit, different form. Look at her audience — mostly middle-class White women. Oprah is their Mammy, telling them which books to read, which diets to follow, which causes to get worked up about. Only difference is that Oprah makes coin because she lives in a more advanced (or different) stage of capitalism than did those who represented Aunt J in minstrel shows a century ago.

Not saying those who don't like rap (code) necessarily hate Black people. Not saying those with Free Tibet stickers (code) dislike Chinese people or Asians in general. Just saying it's human nature to classify and differentiate, to codify and regulate identities. Telling people it's socially unacceptable to call a Chinaman (archetype) a Chinaman (code) doesn't mean people will stop thinking of or treat the Chinaman as a Chinaman, or a Wetback a Wetback, a Dago Wop a Dago Wop. They'll just find a more socially acceptable way to express difference.

The codes and archetypes evolve to reflect the aims and needs of the political economy. Slavery (code) in the US didn't end because enough people *finally* recognized such bondage as immoral. You really think white abolitionists (archetype) gave a shit about "Negroes" anymore than they cared about the "free" Irish immigrants who lived a mile away from them in conditions, according to a University of Chicago economist, even worse than those of Southern slaves? Slavery ended because enough people figured out that it doesn't work well with industrial capitalism. Slavery became immoral because it was becoming inefficient — less productive than wage labor — and not because the temptation to exploit other people in such a way had waned. Just because material life has gotten better and society more civil doesn't mean human nature has changed. People are still scared and vain and will seek short-cuts to the Kingdom of Heaven by trying to create Heaven on Earth, with disastrous consequences. People will forever do some fucked up shit to each other, with most justifying, rationalizing as good and just what they've done, from carpet bombing a village to interrogation by torture to massacre. Instead of burning the witch at the stake, now we post compromising photos of that bitch on Instagram.

History and Human Nature

Why is it we can laugh at or be horrified by instances of human depravity and degeneracy throughout history, yet not recognize our own sins and follies? We can laugh at Ponce DeLeon for being a dumbass for searching for the Fountain of Youth (AND believe in this story which likely isn't true), yet we fall for wheatgrass, spirulina, weight-loss pills, cock enlargement pumps, reverse-aging creams, those metal bracelets that do whatever it is they're supposed to do, and ionized water?

Medical doctors and scientists would probably blame low scientific literacy as the source of the problem. Sure sure, most people don't understand the scientific method or how clinical trials work or the difference between correlation and causation or how problematic observational studies are and what can be concluded from a mice study or what "double blind peer review" means. But I don't think a person needs to be familiar with any of the above to detect bullshit. We have built-in bullshit detectors. We just don't use them.

So why don't we use our bullshit detectors? What makes it so tempting to hear only what we want to hear, to see only what we want to see in ourselves and others? When do we become susceptible to believing fantastic promises that appeal to our vanities?

Part of it is how history is often taught, how we understand it. "Those who cannot remember the past are doomed to repeat it." Thanks for the reminder, George, but forgetting the past isn't the reason why history repeats itself. History repeats itself especially when it's NOT forgotten. Guy sentenced to life in jail for vehicular homicide didn't forget his three DUIs, he was just being human, a dumbass creature of habit. And I'm not claiming "progress" hasn't been made, I'll take my toilet over whatever Jesus used. I'm saying that thinking of the trajectory of history as "moral progress" — qualified by "if we study history" — makes us blind to ourselves, our Original Sin. Unable to see ourselves in Pol Pot, Hitler, Henry V, Catherine the Great, Stalin, Caligula, Judas Iscariot, we become arrogant, vain, self-righteous and self-satisfied. "I would never have owned slaves," the American Apparel clad college girl tells herself as she reads Howard Zinn's *People's History*. "I would've released them, then teach them how to read, to start a glorious revolution." Twenty years later she's living in a nearly Black-less neighborhood, and the closest she's ever come to helping anyone Black has been her purchase of tunes from Aaliyah and a Richard Sherman jersey. How's that for ironic living?

Superfood as Colonial Narrative

Is there an Anthropologist in the house? We're going to need one soon.

(Artistic license taken) "Acai berries for super duper healthy living AND to empower the peasants, save them from greedy capitalists!" In May 2009, Bloomberg reported that the expanding popularity of açaí in the United States was "depriving Brazilian jungle dwellers of a protein-rich nutrient they've relied on for generations." From **Reality Check**: "False claims include reversal of **diabetes** and other **chronic illnesses**, as well as expanding **size of the penis** and increasing men's sexual virility." Oops, we fucked up.

"Quinoa for super duper healthy living AND to empower the peasants, save them from greedy capitalists!" From UK Guardian: "Ethical consumers should be aware poor Bolivians can no longer afford their staple grain, due to western demand raising prices." Oops, we fucked up.

(From Runa website, word for word) "Runa is a social enterprise supporting indigenous farmers and reforestation in the Amazon. Runa brews beverages from **guayusa**, a super-leaf from the Amazon ..." We should know how this "social enterprise" (social fucking enterprise!) is going to end. But we get duped by the same message over and over again: Fountain of Youth! Bigger Penis! Save the Peasants from Greedy Capitalists! We fall for the same pick up line because it makes us feel good, and because deep down, we don't give a shit about those jungle dwelling brown motherfuckers, which is why we can conveniently forget — no, ignore — what happened to them last time we tried to help them. We just like to believe we care about them, and that their big big smiles are for real when they take photos with us. It's as if colonialism never ended. Instead of gold and guns, now the imperialists use superfoods to fuck things up in their own fucked up way. The colonial narrative, that trifecta of: glory and riches, more pussy, and White burden, continues on in American grocery stores and on dining tables.

Here's where an Anthropologist may be of help. Instead of studying how superfood agriculture affects the environment and culture, instead of studying the Other, let's study White people. By White people, I don't mean genotype or White individuals. I mean White people as trope, as inheritors of a colonial legacy. As consumers of *all races* unwilling to recognize the colonial past in their post-colonial present. Let's get to the source of the problem.

History and Human Nature Part II: Self Interest vs. Vanity

Most schools and media teach history as the story about good people as victims of bad people and that we have moral obligation to help the victims of the present and past and punish the bad. Put simply, propaganda. The Aliens watching us from Alpha Centauri don't see good versus evil, they only see people doing fucked up shit to each other, just as we see animals in the wild do fucked up shit to each other but don't assign moral value to their actions. That's precisely the kind of story Thucydides wrote about in *History of the Peloponnesian Wars*. It's a seminal historical text because it's the first to be so cold, detached, impartial; because it isn't a story about good and evil, it's about *human nature* and how we can best protect ourselves from other people. It's a story about how there are NEITHER victims NOR volunteers. There are only competing self-interests that sometimes come in conflict with another.

Santayana's "remember the past so you don't make the same mistakes," is an alluring way to read history because it appeals to our vanity. "Those bad bad people are them, and I'm me, who would never do that, I'm better than that" we're led to think. Really? The only reason why the 19 year old girl who worships Ayn Rand (a Fuck You conservative) can declare herself a Communist (combo = psychobitch, guaranteed) without a hint of irony is because she doesn't have the power to round people up and work them to death at a labor camp. And she's too chickenshit to do anything more than tell her Facebook friends that that bitch is not her mom. Send her back in time — give her power, make her Catherine the Great — then we'll see who she really is. There will be blood everywhere.

If Santayana's version of history takes down the proverbial mirror we need to recognize ourselves in our readings of the past, reading history as the codification of identity and the study of human nature nails it back up for us to see who we really are. With history as the study of human nature on repeat, every cheat, murderer, dumbass, fool, coward, and psychopath we read about becomes a story about our present condition, a reflection of who we are. It helps us recognize our own follies, our venality and arrogance, our total depravity. It may help us to smell present-day bullshit like this:

Ignored since the 1950s -- is Spirulina now a miracle high-protein superfood? Imagine a plant that can nourish your body by providing most of the protein you need to live, help prevent the annoying sniffling and sneezing of allergies, reinforce your immune system, help you control high blood pressure and cholesterol, and help protect you from cancer. Does such a "super food" exist?

Yes. It's called spirulina.

Which isn't much different from bullshit from the past, like this:

SNAKE-OIL LINIMENT
RELIEVES INSTANTANEOUSLY
AND CURES HEADACHE, NEURALGIA, TOOTHACHE, EARACHE, BACKACHE, SWELLINGS, SPRAINS, SORE CHEST, SWELLING of the THROAT, CONTRACTED CORDS and MUSCLES, STIFF JOINTS, WRENCHES, DISLOCATIONS, CUTS and BRUISES.
SNAKE-OIL LINIMENT CURES ALL ACHES AND PAINS.
If You Are Afflicted With DEAFNESS
Get Our Specially Prepared
PURE Rattlesnake Oil

The ingredients may change, but human nature remains.

The Vanity of Vanities

According to Socrates, there are two types of people: dumbasses who know they're dumbasses, and dumbasses who don't. The former ask more questions and make fewer assumptions because of their insecure knowledge. The latter ask few questions and rely on belief, bullshit, and bromides to sustain their vain sense of self. The former go with what sounds right. The latter with what sounds good.

Vanity is self-interest turned on its side, that desire for a sense of progress and self-esteem rather than actual improvement. Pay up and pop the pill to feel like effort and progress has been made, even though it'd cost less and be more effective to consistently eat diverse and balanced meals and to exercise daily. Vanity and its dampening affect on our bullshit detectors, not poor science literacy, is what feeds the pseudoscience and anti-science industries. Michael Schulson, on the importance of keeping our vanity in check when thinking about the politics of science (from **Whole Foods: America's Temple of Pseudoscience**):

It's that whenever we talk about science and society, it helps to keep two rather humbling premises in mind: very few of us are anywhere near rational. And pretty much all of us are hypocrites.

And dumbasses.

ANDREW AN AN HO

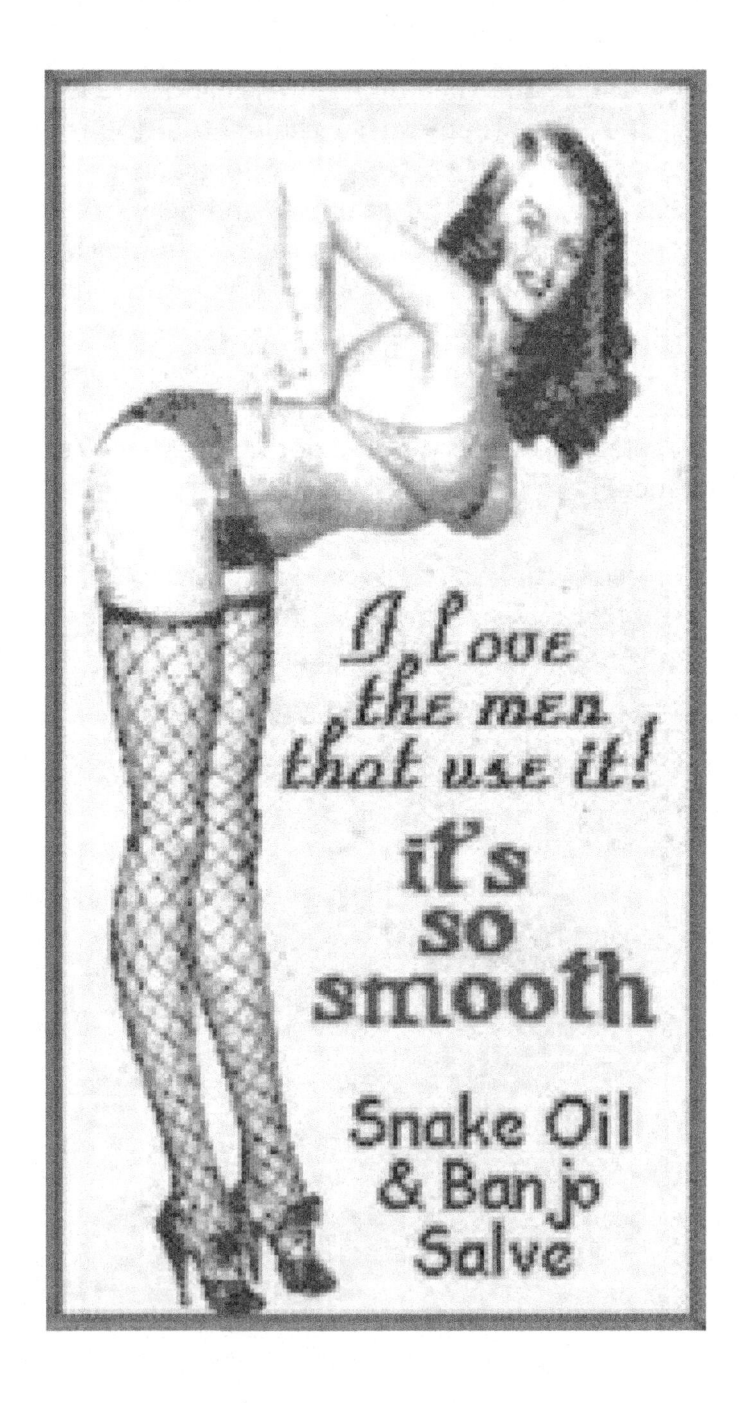

CHAPTER 5 HOW TO EAT WITH INSTINCTS

It's 1973, British couple Maurice and Maralyn Bailey survive 117 days on a rubber life raft in the Pacific. They survived by eating all sorts of sea creatures raw, including turtles. What they craved most during the ordeal were fish eyes and they couldn't figure out why because, like typical Brits, they're grossed out by what Chinese people eat. After their rescue, they learned that fish eyes contain water and vitamin C, both of which they were in dire need of to survive.

If you were lost at sea, you'd eat those eyes.

Point of the story is that we're able to eat with our instincts and intuition — our bodies *can* tell us when and what to eat instead of eating when and what we're told to eat. And when you're in survival mode, these instincts override all cultural habits, including aversion to really nasty Chinese food. You'll eat what you need to eat to survive.

How to Eat With Instincts and Intuition

Instincts we're born with, while intuition is developed based on experiences. Not saying intuition is always correct — it's often wrong — but it can be honed and enhanced with enough introspection.

Keep in mind that we're taught, especially in school, to not trust our instincts and to not develop our intuition. We're told, for instance, to not trust our own eyes *because our experiences are anecdotal and therefore mean jack shit*. And that only so-called experts can interpret the world for us.

Below are steps to reverse what we've been taught.

Step 1: Activate your instincts. Do sports — yoga and dance count — to activate instincts. The stress and sense of immediacy from playing sports with high intensity takes you closer to survival mode so that you become more aware of your body signals. Listen for the dialogue between what your body wants and what your mind craves. The body in survival mode wants nutrition and instinctively knows where to find it, while the disturbed mind seeks immediate comfort (eg pint of ice cream). You get sick when your mind isn't aligned with what your body wants.

Step 2: Question every habit and idea you think is normal and natural. Do one a week. Examples:

- Is sitting in chair healthier than squatting?
- Is Western democracy the best form of government for all nations?
- Should I drink orange juice when I have the flu?
- Does school make people smarter or dumber?
- Are polite people good people?
- How often and when should I eat?

Give yourself a week to investigate the debates, it'll be a mind opening experience. The more you question your assumptions — cultural biases taught in school and by mainstream media — the more your instincts and intuition will kick in and tell you who is full of shit. Insanity is when those who are lactose intolerant (70 percent of world population) keep drinking cow milk just because the government says you need to to be healthy. Listen to your body, listen to the sound of diarrhea, not to so-called experts with bullshit degrees.

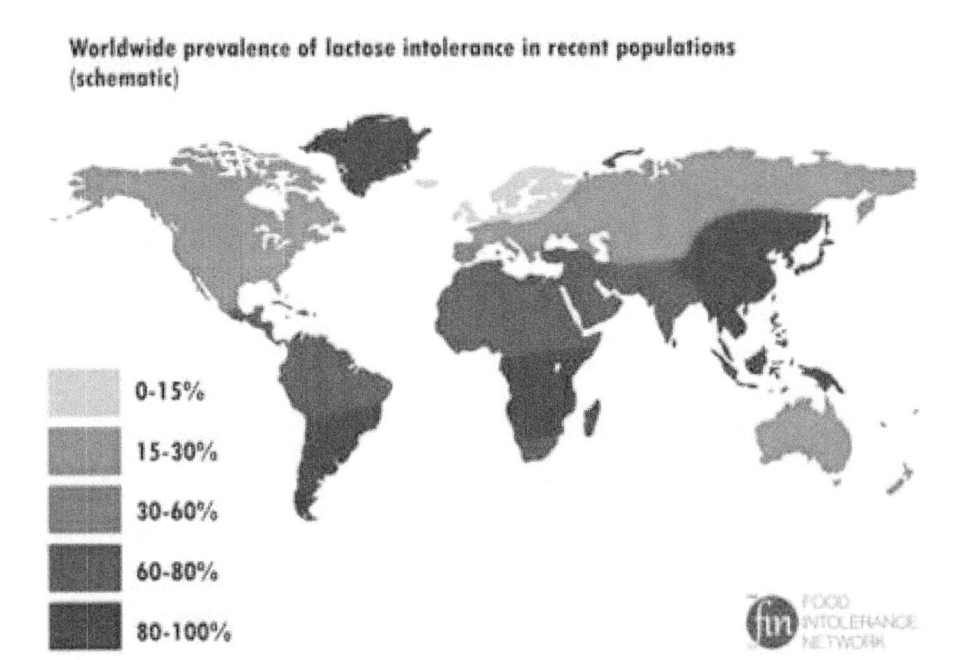

Worldwide prevalence of lactose intolerance in recent populations (schematic)

- 0-15%
- 15-30%
- 30-60%
- 60-80%
- 80-100%

FOOD INTOLERANCE NETWORK

Are government nutritionists paid off by dairy lobby, or are they just Anglo-centric nitwits?

Step 3: Watch stand-up comedy. Stand-up comedians are the most intuitive social critics around. They say what we feel and think intuitively but are afraid to express for fear of offending. In Anglo-centric cultures, where politeness is lauded as a virtue, stand-up comedians are one of the few with the courage to tell the truth. Hearing the truth about who you and other people are will help you develop your intuition, which is your ability to recognize patterns to make sense of experiences. For instance, I've learned from experience to never trust overly polite people — they are vile, incompetent, and socially inept — even though I was taught that politeness is a sign of good breeding. A recent study **by the Association for Computational Linguistics supports my intuition**. Sure, you'll be called a racist and sexist and whatever else they come up with for challenging what you've been taught, but you'll be a lot closer to and better prepared for the truth.

Stand-up comedian Russell Peters tells racist jokes. Pay attention to his observations, and not to what dumbfuck Ethnic Studies professors have to say.

Put simply, stand up comedians remind you of what the world is, which protects you from falling in love with your version of how the world ought to be. Stand up comedy trains you to trust your guts — which tells you the truth — and never your heart, which only tells you what you want to hear.

That's why you should watch Ronny Chieng. He reminds you of how insignificant you are, which is a lot closer to the truth than the snowflake bullshit you learn in school.

Step 4: Do as kids do, they're cuter versions of stand-up comedians. We're taught it's uncivilized to live instinctively and rude to develop our intuition. Watch pre-kindergarten kids in Anglo nations, they instinctively squat to sit, as do most adults in the non-Western world. They also eat instinctively: instead of using a spoon, they'll bring a bowl of soup to their mouths, as do most adults in the non-Western world. They communicate instinctively, they're blunt and ask lots of questions, are never euphemistic and don't care if they offend. They don't practice bizarre manners and habits until their instincts are beaten out of them, often at school.

According to anthropologists, this is the healthy and instinctive way to sit and eat, and this is how it's done through most of the world. Yet most American adults can't do this because they've been programmed to sit in chairs that ruin their backs and hamstrings instead.

I single out Anglo-nations for promoting this kind of civility that's neither natural nor found in most cultures. The point of doing so is to emphasize that cultures are as malleable as they are enduring and how we live *isn't* necessarily normal or natural, even if it feels that way to us. My aim here, at best, is to suggest that we don't have to live this way. We can instead strive to live as God intended us to live before the Fall.

CHAPTER 6 HOW TO ORDER THE NASTY SHIT

Wonder what Chinese people eat? Curious about how you can get some of it? Want to try to act Chinese and eat some of the nasty shit?

Three types of Chinese restaurants.

1. Those that cater exclusively to Foreign Devils (aka Gweilo, that's probably you and if it isn't, go back to eating your nasty shit). They serve food like sweet and sour pork, General Tso Chicken, beef and broccoli, and fortune cookies. Dishes invented in the US. Not saying there's anything wrong with these dishes (I especially like beef and broccoli). Though the fortune cookie is bizarre.

2. Those that cater to Foreign Devils and those who speak Chinese. Foreign Devils get English menu; others the Chinese menu. English menu similar to what you'd find at restaurants that cater exclusively to Foreign Devils, but includes dishes that originate from China. Chinese menu offers nasty shit.

3. Those that cater primarily to Chinese. Only a Chinese menu.

Serves lots of nasty shit.

What's the Nasty Shit?

Some examples:

1. Jellyfish. Slightly crunchy, sliced into noodles, usually drenched in a sauce. Barbarians who try it mistake it for a vegetable.

2. Beef intestine (tripe). Also slightly crunchy in texture, sliced into noodles. Soaked in a mild sauce.

3. Stinky tofu. Fermented in some really nasty shit, so it stinks. Those who first encounter it may feel as if they're locked in a 4×4 room with two guys farting nonstop after a been and milk meal. Be patient, stick with it. When you acquire taste for it, it'll smell like your own fart. Or your own feet. Stinky but oddly pleasurable, enticing. Addictive. You'll want more.

4. Duck tongue. Yes, it's possible.

5. Chicken feet. Fun to eat, get it at any place that serves dim sum. Slow cooked in a sauce, the bones break off easily. You play with them in your mouth, using your tongue to strip off the meat. Then spit out the bones. This is how I learned to kiss before my first kiss.

6. Fish eyeballs.

7. Fish heads. That's why we keep the head on. We plan on eating it.

8. Duck head. That's why we keep the head on. We plan on gnaw-

ing on it.

9. Pig's colon. Don't worry, the caca has been washed out. And even if it hasn't, it's thoroughly cooked. No worries, I promise. Sheesh.

10. Pig uterus. Why toss it, waste it? Cook it in some soy sauce, slice it up. It's like Chinese calamari.

How to Get the Nasty Shit

First, you've got to convince your server that you're ready for the nasty shit. If you speak Chinese, they'll give it to you. If you don't, they'll hesitate, and in some cases, not give you what you order (give you fried rice and orange chicken instead). Be persistent. Have what you want written on paper, English is fine in restaurants that serve both Foreign Devils and Chinese. If you're in a restaurant that serves mostly Chinese people, use sign language. Make a claw (with hand, not feet) if you want chicken feet. Point to stomach if you want beef tripe. Squeeze your nose if you want stinky tofu. Make fish lips and point to eyes if you want fish eyes. Do it. Do it. It works. But don't point at your asshole if you want pig colon. Trust me on this one, too much room for misunderstanding.

Most of the body parts above are also served throughout Europe, South America, and Africa. Question arises: if most of the world eats offals and this ingredient and that body part served in this and that way, how did the American palate develop to become so limited? It wasn't always this way and has since become much more inclusive. To explore how the mainstream American palate was developed after WWII is to ask questions about the politics of food and eating and the psychology of nation-building.

CHAPTER 7 WHY WE EAT WHAT WE EAT

Thorstein Veblen publishes *Theory of the Leisure Class: an Economic Study of Institutions* in 1899. He's trying to figure out what makes people act like douchebags by studying their consumption habits. Like why Sara buys clothes at this store; Marty drives that car; Vivian drinks obscure coffee. Pre-test:

1. Who owns a Corvette?

a) Vascular Surgeon

b) The commercial plumber

c) The tenured college professor

2. Who owns most amount of clothes?

a) White trash girl living in trailer park

b) Old money girl attending exclusive boarding school

c) Middle-class girl living in middle-class cul-de-sac

3. What does middle-class woman eat on her birthday?

a) Surf and turf

b) Sushi and tempura

c) Raw oysters and beef tongue

4. What is upper-class woman eating Friday evening?

a) Cocktail shrimp and beef tenderloin steak

b) Acai bowl with quinoa, kale chips on side

c) Grilled beef tongue and fried shrimp heads

5. Who is most likely to have read a violent pornographic novel (eg. Georges Bataille, Pauline Reage, Marquis de Sade)

a) Upper-class woman, undergrad from Wellesley and PhD in Comparative Literature

b) Middle-class home economics teacher with enormous porn collection.

c) White trash who beats the shit out of his girlfriend.

Answers:

1. b

2. c

3. a

4. c

5. a

Surprised? Oblique explanations in main text.

Why People Act Like Poseurs and Douchebags

For our purposes here, the only thing we need to take from *Theory of Leisure Class* is that imitation is the driving force of American capitalist consumerism. In Feudalism, social mobility is limited by birth and the serf works for subsistence, not social mobility. Capitalism, promising unprecedented (upward and downward) social mobility, makes imitation possible, accessible, and encouraged by the logic of economic growth. "Keeping up," as Americans put it. The capitalist "Leisure Class" signifies not only Old and New Money, but anyone with discretionary income, or at least anyone with a credit card.

Whom do people imitate? Those they *perceive* as just above them. What do people imitate? The *imagined* sensibilities and habits of those they *perceive* as just above them. Pay attention to the choice of words: "perceive" and "imagined" because people from all social classes tend to have trouble at not only figuring out what those outside their social circles are thinking and doing, but also a person's social status. That's why the not-quite-middle-class teen thinks the woman with a deep tan and a tit job is high society. The Old Money woman thinks the young tow truck driver is being ironic when he's not. The woman who reads The New Yorker has no idea who Jimmie Johnson is. The guy with collection of Jimmie Johnson autographs can't imagine an Ivy League college professor who listens to Outkast and has tickets to Venus in Furs and The Vagina

HOW TO EAT LIKE AN ASSHOLE

Monologues, both of which the Time and Oprah magazine reading home economics teacher with tickets to The Nutcracker Suite finds dirty and offensive. Which is why all this imitation looks more like self-parody than "faking it till you make it."

History of American Cuisine: Colonial Era

Pick:

6. What's most likely on the menu at a two year old casual fine dining restaurant in New York City that just won its first Micheline star?

a) Lobster alfredo with chantrelle mushrooms

b) Bone marrow with jerk spiced duck hearts

c) Wagyu tenderloin served with roasted rosemary potatoes

7. Who sucked the most dick by age 18?

a) Working middle-class Tina who attended Catholic school

b) Upper-middle class Siobhan who attended exclusive boarding school

c) Working middle-class Anthony who attended public school

8. Which family is most likely to own Emily Post books on etiquette and send children to etiquette school?

a) Conservative middle-class family, mom is homemaker, dad is bank manager.

b) Old Money family, mom is art curator, dad is opera singer.

c) New Money Google millionaires, Mom and Dad are executives

9. Who sucked the most dick by age 28?

a) Working middle-class Tina who attended Catholic school

b) Upper-middle class Siobhan who attended exclusive boarding school

c) Old Money Sarah who attended public school

10. What vehicle does single Korean man who runs with his parents an established Teriyaki store drive?

a) Toyota Camry

b) Ford Mustang

c) Porsche Cayenne

Answers:

6. b

7. a

8. a

9. b

10. c

Seventeenth century, White Europeans from varied backgrounds started moving to The New World. The English soon became dominant, assimilating the Dutch and the Swedes after kicking their asses, but they couldn't reach a deal with the French (Acadians in Nova Scotia) so the English told them to fuck off, relocating some of them to Louisiana where they begin Cajun culture. Point is, American cuisine began as a variant of British cuisine, and in contrast to the French, who adopted Native American hunting and cooking methods and incorporated indigenous ingredients into their diet, the Americans used Old World Methods to prepare New World ingredients and tried to grow Old World ingredients in New World climate, with mixed results. Where reliable trade with British Empire was established, Old World ingredients were imported, making American (New England especially) cuisine intentionally British.

There were lots of regional variations that cut across socio-economic lines — American cuisine has never been monolithic — with, for instance, upland Southern Rednecks eating possums and squirrels with cabbage and potatoes, and African and Caribbean ingredients and cooking methods influencing the pork based lowland Southern diet. Pennsylvania Germans brought sausages, sauerkraut, and beer from the Old World. But colonial British mercantilist policies that limited American trade to within the Empire ensured that British traditions would dominate until the Brits began taxing alcohol starting with the Molasses Act of 1733 and the Sugar Act of 1760, and then luxury goods with the Quartering Act of 1763 and tea with the Tea Act of 1773.

The Brits soon learned that when you fuck with people's alcohol and caffeine supply, there's going to be a revolution. Americans began boycotting British goods and finally went native out of frustration with British laws. Whiskey had been looked down on by American high society types, who preferred Old World British goods and habits. Now Northern whiskey, made of rye (non-native European ingredient), was becoming fashionable, and Southern whiskey was considered patriotic due to its use of corn, an indigenous ingredient. Rum was out, as it was seen as a symbol of British power.

Another significant change was the shift from tea to coffee. John Adams wrote to his wife in 1773: "Tea must be universally renounced and I must be weaned, and the sooner the better." When word got out that a group of housewives in Massachusetts united to serve — as a fuck you to the Brits — only coffee, many were inspired to do the same.

It's been said that you can tell a lot about a person by what he or she eats. We can probably tell a lot about a nation by what its people eat. Shifts in eating habits aren't accidents and they're an index of what's to come politically. You can smell a revolution that's waiting to happen.

Independence – Immigration Act of 1924

Independence achieved, Americans stopped shitting on French cuisine, which they had disdained during the seemingly never ending conflict between the British and the French. Before the War, cookbook writer Hannah Glasse, wrote in *Art of Cookery*: "the blind folly of this age that would rather be imposed on by a French booby, than give encouragement to a good English cook!" On French recipes: "an odd jumble of trash." Those insults disappeared in the first *American* post-war edition of her cookbook, probably because the French had helped with American war effort. The French-American alliance also led to French chefs migrating to the States during the French Revolution, which would've been unthinkable under British rule.

Free from the constraints of British mercantilism, American cooks gained wider access to foreign goods. As an expanding industrializing nation requiring more White people (1790 Act limited citizenship to White people) to populate conquered lands and to work in expanding factories, the US began to accept more and a wider range of White immigrants — now including many from Eastern and Southern Europe — who further diversified American culinary habits. By 1924, Americans are eating all kinds of peasant-redneck-soul food — pig's ears, raw oysters, raw beef, possums, ram testicles, squirrels, chicken gizzards, cow brains, pig's feet, and blood pudding.

I use year 1924 as a bookend because it marks the end of liberal immigration policies and the beginning of the modern kitchen. Growing concern about the "Whiteness" of some European immigrants — Italians, Slavs, and Eastern European Jews — the Immigration Act of 1924 limited the annual number of immigrants who could be admitted from any country to 2% of the number of people from that country who were already living in the US. It was a way to ensure that the US remained a White, Anglo-Saxon, Protestant (WASP) nation, not overrun by Irish and Italian Catholics, Jews, Slavs, and other undesirable not-quite-White European "races." And by severing the flow of people and cultural habits from undesirable parts of Europe to ethnic US neighborhoods, the not-quite-White people of the US would finally lose their immigrant heritage and assimilate to become fully White and American.

And it was around 1924 that modern refrigeration was becoming common in middle-class America, which led to the rise to mass produced industrialized foods such as frozen meals. Refrigeration in rail cars meant farms no longer had to be located near population centers and more land could be farmed, resulting in lower prices of prestige items such as beef.

The Federal government and academia were also getting involved in what Americans ate. Nutritionists and home economics professors introduced a scientific approach to nutrition and eating. They began telling Americans which meals and cooking methods are safe and proper.

Modern American Cuisine

Why did some American ethnic and regional foods become popular nationally, while others remained marginalized or disappeared?

Test break!

11. Who sucked the most dick by age 45?

a) Working middle-class Tina who attended Catholic school

b) Upper-middle class Siobhan who attended exclusive boarding school

c) Old Money Sarah who attended public school

12. It's 1973, in some middle to upper middle class suburb. What do the Johnson's have in their kitchen?

a) A dead body, cut up, probably neighbor's daughter

b) White Wonder bread, margarine, and Tang.

c) Pickled beets, sauerkraut, and offals.

13. Where has Old Money Sarah never eaten?

a) McDonald's

b) Harold's Chicken Shack

c) Red Lobster

14. Who lost a toe while on vacation?

a) Upper middle-class Ginger

b) Lower-middle class Tiffany

c) Upper-class Wes

15. Who spends the most on nails and tan?

a) Old Money Sarah

b) Upper middle-class Jimmy

c) Lower-middle class Tiffany

Answers:

11. a

12. b

13. c

14. c

15. c

By 1965, the year immigration was liberalized, the US had finally developed a national cuisine and palate. Coca Cola, orange juice, hamburgers, fortune cookies, peanut butter, apple pie, fried chicken, hot dog, steak, pizza, french fries, spaghetti... these are some regional foods that went national (a few, like Coca Cola, went international). Why not mutton, smoked salmon, collard greens, pig trotters, fried gizzards, baklava, gyros, Philly Cheesesteaks, and knishes?

Some food became less had because eating them was a sign of low status. Offals (organs) and possum, for instance. Perhaps fried chicken made the cut because it was special occasion food for the poor, and fried gizzards didn't because that's what the poor ate everyday. Those who grew up poor traded liver, horse meat, and beef intestines for ground beef when they finally could.

Some food became more popular because they represented modernity and science. The middle-class household in 1970 drank space-age Tang to be modern, used margarine instead of butter to be health conscious, and ate canned soup to be family-on-the-move efficient. Now Tang is one step above kool-aid, margarine is for out-of-touch geriatrics relying on out-of-date info, and canned soup is for the lazy.

Other food and preparation methods became rare because of warnings from government agencies. "You shouldn't consume raw seafood or meat of any kind," warns the FDA. So most stopped doing so, even as steak tartare was served throughout

Europe, as it had for centuries, and sashimi throughout Japan, as it had for centuries. You're supposed to drink cow milk and eat cereal and bread and cheese…everyday "we're told by USDA food pyramid. So we did, even though 70 percent of the people in the world are lactose intolerant. "Cook poultry at 350 degrees," taught the home economics teacher. We did and learned to make overcooked and dry meat palatable by adding to it extra extra gravy. "White meat is healthier than dark meat," announced the nutritionist. So we became one of the few nations in the world to prefer white over dark, even though dark is more flavorful and moister. (And then we make white meat better tasting by frying it or drenching it in gravy, making it even more calorie dense than its dark counterpart). Americans were being taught to distrust their immigrant heritage, to become more modern (American) and less ethnic (backward). American cuisine was narrowing palates and limiting the range of cooking methods. American cuisine was becoming a disaster.

Thesis: government meddling and the loss of immigrant heritage fucked up American cuisine.

Postmodern American Cuisine

If Modernity is about living as one imagines one would in the future, Postmodernity is about living as one imagines someone had in the past.

The Japanese, not Julia Child, saved American cuisine.

It's the 1980s and the Japanese are on a roll. Americans are starting to think the Japanese are going to take over the world. They show up in Manhattan to buy all sorts of vanity properties, their cars run better than American ones, and they make Americans feel lazy, and stupid. One could smell the power shift when business between Japanese and Americans was conducted not at Peter Luger steakhouse, but in a basement level izakaya.

The growing popularity of Japanese cuisine in the US during the 80s and 90s gave Americans an opportunity to reconsider everything they'd been taught about proper cooking and proper meals. Sure sure, there were American servicemen who loved Japanese cuisine before the preppy douchebags got to try it, but these were working class types everyone ignored, not the preppies middle-class kids emulated during the materialistic Eighties. The preppies made Japanese food cool and eating it became a sign of sophistication and high social status.

Soon Americans are watching Iron Chef Japan. Eating raw fish. Now they're trying eel and loving it. A few even develop a taste for natto and live sea urchin. Everything Americans were *told not to do they were doing when they were eating Japanese food.* For some, it was exhilarating. Trying "weird" food became a legitimate hobby, and a new brand of foodie emerged.

By the start of the 21st century, Japanese cuisine had gone mainstream and Japanese cooking shows like Iron Chef inspired American versions of them, transforming chefs into rock stars, Ivy League graduates into line cooks working to become chefs, and cooking into a hobby instead of a chore. Sushi was no longer for Wall Street pricks and Californian champagne socialists, you were not middle-class if you didn't eat and like sushi (even though sushi is a small portion of Japanese cuisine, and not very often in Japan). Soon we had Japanese food for the masses: conveyor belt sushi, all you can eat sushi, even Chinese people serving (disgusting) sushi. And as Japanese food ceased to be the new in thing, White Americans, now accustomed to trying "weird shit," became interested in rediscovering their European roots because being White wasn't cool anymore. More restaurants started serving dishes that would've been unthinkable in the mainstream 70s, from raw oysters to bone marrow, duck hearts to steak tartare; using cooking methods, such as sous vide, that freaked out health inspectors. Underground dinner parties featured beef tongue and shrimp head. Eating such dishes became a sign of sophistication and American cuisine was becoming not just an archetype of postmodern nostalgia, but also vibrant and challenging. For the first time in a long time, American palates and culinary repertoire were expanding and a new generation of American chefs wanted to show the world that there's more to American cuisine than McDonald's.

Why We Eat What We Eat

Some think that the standard middle-class American cuisine is based primarily on proper nutrition (as determined by government agencies) and ethical behavior (as determined by soft science academics). It is not. If it were, we'd be eating crickets instead of beef for protein and we wouldn't let ourselves get suckered by the latest health fad that confers an ingredient undeserved powers and fucks up another nation's ecology. Some of us would like to believe our cuisine is *proper* because it justifies our personal preferences (built on habit) and confirms our sense of self as belonging to a righteous nation. Those unhappy with status quo want to make American cuisine *proper* — nutritious and ethical (eg. locavore movement) — so we can feel like we belong to a righteous nation.

If American cuisine is, as argued earlier, built on political intrigue, social maneuvering, and economic brinkmanship, then there's a good chance that its present is an expression of our competing political beliefs and anxiety about our socio-economic future. Reading the food we eat as such makes it possible for us to see ourselves as tools when we drink orange juice every morning for its Vitamin C content, douchebags when we order kobe burgers for the prized fat that's cooked off, cranks when we promote acai berries as ethical superfood, and human when we binge on McDonald's fries.

Perhaps in the end — weary of reading all those conflicting articles about what's healthiest and what's more ethical and what's better for the economy and environment — eating well has less to do with what we eat than *how we explore what's possible to eat*. If only God can determine the righteousness of a nation and its citizens, the best we can do is build a spirited cuisine that challenges and expands, rather than accepts and limits, our palates and imagination.

CHAPTER 8 WHY PEOPLE PREFER BAD SERVICE

For the same reason the drunk sailor mistakes the tranny for a woman. For the same reason people like bad writing: some mistake pompous service for good service just as they mistake pompous writing (aka purple prose) for good writing. Here's an example of bad service that people think as good service, from social critic Mark Randall (from Not That You Asked):

"Good evening, sir…And how are you this evening?…May I get you something from the bar? …I'd be happy to, sir….And would you care for anything else right now?…I'll be back with your drink in just a moment."

Randall describes such service as:

…superfluous little phrases…but as they pile up they begin to irritate with their pretentiousness. One realizes that they do not add to the service or quicken it. They do not even make it more pleasant since one is forced (out of politeness) to parry each one of these pointless and limpid thrusts.

Another social critic, Paul Fussell calls that shit "pretentious greasy-smarmy rhetoric of the servitors." It's like bad porn, watching a guy eat pussy as if he's eating a hot dog. There's the ridiculous use of "Sir" to suggest to the customer that at that moment, he is a feudal lord and his serfs are at his command, ready to do anything — anything — he wants them to do. Then there are the stupid questions or questions phrased stupidly. And finally, the unnecessary comments. That's why Randall is pissed:

One wants to say, 'well of course you'll be back with my drink in a moment! SHUT UP ABOUT IT!'

Randall, on the purpose of pretentious service:

One sees…that this style is designed, not to promote service, but to call attention to what we are supposed to regard as the edifyingly refined manner of the server. It is the establishment's self-congratulatory way of reminding you that you are in a fancy place….What we have here is neither good manners nor good service; it is politeness grandstanding, a kind of obsequious bullying.

This "bullying" is similar to what people do when they want others to think that they have a lot of money. They pull the same shit, except instead of meaningless words they use meaningless bling, clothes, and cars to communicate what they may or may not have. Some have money, many are frauds. Many of those who practice "politeness grandstanding" are similar frauds, using unnecessary or stupid words and phrases to create the impression of sophistication and class when in fact they're simply putting on airs.

What is Good Service?

Good service is similar to good writing. Less is more, elegance

HOW TO EAT LIKE AN ASSHOLE

in simplicity, and stay focused on the job. Good writing is effective communication — clear, concise, and precise — never self-indulgent by showing off vocabulary or writing dramatic prose (aka purple prose) because it's always focused on the topic. Good service is about giving what the customer wants with precision and alacrity without violating your integrity (don't act like serf ready to suck dick unless that's what you want or are paid to do). Good service doesn't rely on flattery, and it's not garrulous, intrusive, or unnecessarily formal. It's observant, helpful, and insightful. Good service is convivial and conviviality is a Redneck virtue. Randall on Redneck conviviality:

...an American friendly style, one that is outgoing and engaging. It is, I believe, an authentic national characteristic. The new "luxury" style though is a hybrid bastard, one that tries to combine American friendliness with European formality.

When you combine Redneck conviviality with middle-class putting on airs, you get embarrassing results. The self-indulgent garrulous and formal exchanges waste time, increasing costs. Randall again:

What one gets is a style that's too friendly to be formal, and too formal to be friendly. It consists entirely of a dozen or so phrases, premeditated, flatulent, pseudo high-class, none of which improve upon "good morning..." thank you," and "you're welcome."

American middle-class politeness may not be rude, but it may be bad manners and certainly is bad taste. Curmudgeon Paul Fussell on why middle-class Americans talk like this:

The middles cleave to euphemisms not just because they're an aid in avoiding facts. They like them also because they assist their social yearnings towards pomposity. This is possible because most eu-

phemisms permit the speaker to multiply syllables, and the middle class confuses sheer numerousness with weight and value.

And good manners.

Examples of Bad Writing

There are several Bad Writing contests, one which invites writers to submit their own worst first sentence for a novel. Here's one that won in 2008:

Theirs was a New York love, a checkered taxi ride burning rubber, and like the city, their passion was open 24/7, steam rising from their bodies like slick streets exhaling warm, moist breath through manhole covers stamped "Forged by DeLaney Bros.

Overwrought and pretentious. An example of author preening and of self-indulgent writing. Yet some are impressed with this passage simply because of its use of metaphors, however inane and vacant they may be.

There's a lot of bad writing in academia too, especially in disciplines that have inferiority complex. UC Berkeley Comp Lit professor Judith Butler won an award for bad academic writing in 1998. The winning sentence (don't try to read all of it, it'll ruin your day):

The move from a structuralist account in which capital is understood to structure social relations in relatively homologous ways to a view of hegemony in which power relations are subject to repetition, convergence, and rearticulation brought the question of temporality into the thinking of structure, and marked a shift from a form of Althusserian theory that takes structural totalities as theoretical ob-

jects to one in which the insights into the contingent possibility of structure inaugurate a renewed conception of hegemony as bound up with the contingent sites and strategies of the rearticulation of power.

Translation: "Stop looking down on me, Math/Physics/Engineering profs who unfairly make twice as much as I do. Comparative Lit. major is just as difficult and important and my writing is tougher to understand than multivariable calculus, so fuck you." Yet many think the author is intelligent and erudite simply because the passage is impenetrable.

Bad service uses similar gimmicks, intimidation tactics really. When the person serving you sounds like a muppet or talks like a pompous academic, don't show approval. Approval is why there's so much bad service. And encouraging people to be frauds is bad for them and society. That's how batshit crazy starts and there's a lot of batshit crazy in middle-class America, the most medicated demographic in the world.

Randall on why Americans enjoy bad service:

The American corporation, no doubt with the aid of market research, has taken something that ought to have been...pleasurable and simple and made it self-serving, burdensome, and complicated. No wonder we're not very polite even when even the experts can't get it right, when politeness becomes this insipid and interminable fugue of gratuitous endearments and self-flattering concern.

Put simply, bad service is narcissism disguised as good service.

Which do you prefer, rude service or bad service? They're not the same.

Examples Good Service and Good Customers

(At random sit-down restaurant, first time customer arrives)

Server: Good evening. Something to drink?

Customer: Jack Daniels straight.

Server: One Jack Daniels straight.

Customer: Yes.

Server: Anything else?

Customer: Maybe, I'll look over the menu.

Note: This is how normal people communicate. The conciseness means fewer communication errors.

(At Alive Juice Bar, regular customer enters)

Server: Hey Susan!

Customer: Hey! Summer Berries.

Server: One Summer Berries.

Customer: Yep!

Server: Summer Berries, ready! Haven't seen you in awhile, how have you been?

Customer: yada yada yada yada and how have you been?

Note: Good service begins with acknowledgment, followed by giving what customer wants. Personal talk is last because that's not primary reason customer is at store. Unless customer is trying to hook up with server.

Examples of Bad Service and Bad Customers

(At random sit-down restaurant)

Server: Hello and good evening, sir. My name is Rodney and I'll be your server this evening. How are you this evening, sir?

Customer: I'm doing rather well, thank you. And how are you this lovely evening?

Server: I'm doing great, thanks for asking. Can I start you with something to drink?

Customer: Yes, I'd like a Jack Daniels, straight, please and if you don't mind.

Server: Oh no, I don't mind at all. I'll be right back with that for you.

Customer: Thank you very much.

Server: Oh you're welcome

Note: Polite small talk is poor sign that someone is a decent person. According to one study, serial killers excel at polite small talk. That's why they're able to get away with killing so many people.

(Alive Juice Bar)

Server: Hi, how are you?

Customer: I'm great, thank you! How are you?

Server: I'm doing well. Wow, you look great in that skirt. Where did you get it, if you don't mind me asking?

Customer: Awww, thanks! I got it at Biji's.

Server: Thanks! What can I get for you this evening?

Customer: Can I please have a Summer Berries when you get a chance?

Server: Excellent choice maam, I'll get that started for you.

Note: Flattery is douchebag and obsequious way to get a bigger tip, like a guy trying to fuck a woman. Save it for after the transaction is completed so it doesn't come off as flattery. That is, manipulation. Server should instead focus on doing a good job.

Examples of What Happens When You Refuse to Play Along

(At random sit-down restaurant)

Server (voice an octave higher than usual, bubbly and sweet) : Hello sir, welcome to Claim Jumper. My name is Ruby and I'll be your server this evening. How are you this evening?

Customer: Jack Daniels, straight.

Server: (confused pause). Excellent choice, sir, I'll get that out for you, just give me a sec.

Server: Here you go, your Jack Daniels. Have you had a chance to read over the menu?

Customer: Fish and chips.

Server: Fish and chips, excellent choice, sir. Would you like anything else with that?

Customer: I'd like a side-order of suck my dick.

Server: Excuse me?

Customer: I said I'd like a side-order of suck my dick. Because you sound like you want to suck my dick while I eat my fish and chips.

Server: (pauses and looks shocked) uh, pardon me, I'll be back.

Manager: Hello and good evening sir. How are you this evening?

Customer: Hungry and horny.

Manager: Now, if I may ask, what did you order?

Customer: Fish and chips and a side order of suck my dick.

Manager: (pauses and looks shocked) Sir, I'm going to have to ask you to leave and never come back, if you don't mind.

Note the number of vacant phrases — eg. "if you don't mind," "if I may ask" used by customer service. And why does the customer need to know the server's name if he's not planning on meeting her again? If he does want to meet her again, he'll ask for her name.

(At Alive Juice Bar)

Server: Hey!

Customer (on her way to past juice bar to dance studio): Hi, how are you?

Server: Do you care?

Customer (stops): Yes, as a matter of fact, I do!

Server: Then why were you walking away from me instead of sitting down to talk to me?

Customer (pauses): Ooook. I'll be right back to talk to you. I just have to drop this off in the dance studio.

Server: Ok.

HOW TO EAT LIKE AN ASSHOLE

Chinaman in the middle is Edsel Fong. Known as the rudest waiter in America. But at least he didn't give bad service.

72

CHAPTER 9 WHY BEING NICE WILL KILL YOU

From a **2008 Journal of Immunotoxicology** article:

"Risk of developing certain diseases correlates with human personality."

Specifically, the authors are matching health with coping styles, active versus passive.

Summary of four personality types, A-D, plus how each type thinks about food:

Type A: The Angry Motherfucker

- Driven
- Fast Paced
- Assertive and Demanding
- Sloppy diet, eats whatever is convenient.
- Food as fuel.

Type B: The Stoner

- Laid back
- Prone to procrastination
- Relaxed
- Expansive diet, eats whatever tastes good.
- Food as pleasure

Type C: The Nice One

- *Passive*
- *Sensitive*
- *Polite*
- *Cycle of dieting and overeating*
- *Food as addiction (emotional eater)*

Type D: The Worrier

- Distressed
- Anxious
- Fearful
- Frequently tries strict, fad, and crash diets.
- Food as poison (obsessed about dangers of eating this or that).

Type As are susceptible to coronary disease and heart attacks. Type Bs will die from falling off the roof while drunk and stoned at a party. Type Cs are most likely to contract autoimmune diseases. Type D, being as stressed out as Type As and as depressed as Type Cs, are fucked.

From **Psyche Central**, on Type C personality:

In recent years, a cluster of personality characteristics has come to be identified as the Type C personality, someone who is at heightened risk for a slew of afflictions, from colds to asthma to **cancer**. *In contrast with the Type A person (who angers easily and has difficulty keeping feelings under wraps) and the Type B person (who has* *a healthier balance of emotional expressiveness), the Type C person is a suppressor, a stoic, a denier of feelings. He or she has a calm, outwardly rational, and unemotional demeanor, but also a tendency to conform to the wishes of others, a lack of assertiveness, and an inclination toward feelings of helplessness or hopelessness.*

Examples: she hates football but pretends to like it to attract more men. He doesn't want to work the holidays but always agrees to do so with an insincere smile. She hates her haircut but won't tell the hairdresser he fucked up because she doesn't want to risk hurting his feelings. He doesn't like his food but won't complain about it until he gets home and unleashes his anger anonymously on yelp. She won't call her husband the lazy piece of shit he is because she's conflict adverse. There's a lot of quiet stewing going on here.

The above cited description of Type C can be more nuanced. It's not that Type C denies feelings (and thoughts), they deny *specific feelings and thoughts,* which in the American socio-cultural context typically means anger and hate, murder and mutilation.

Canadian physician Gabor Mate...began to notice a pattern: individuals who were unable to express anger, who didn't seem to recognize the primacy of their own needs, and who were constantly doing for others, appeared to be the ones most susceptible to a slew of ailments, from asthma, rheumatoid arthritis, and lupus to multiple sclerosis and amyotrophic lateral sclerosis. These conditions are all autoimmune disorders. Mate claims that, when an individual engages in a long-term practice of ignoring or suppressing legitimate feelings–when he or she is just plain too nice–the immune system can become compromised and confused, learning to attack the self rather than defend it.

Again, we need more nuance, as above description makes it seem as if nice people are martyrs. They're not, some of them are raging narcissists who write purple prose, Albert Camus reminds us in *The Fall* (aka Confessions of a Nice Guy). That tension, that dissonance between the inner narcissist and the outer martyr means there's going to be a lot of ice cream and chocolate to medicate depression. Which is why some personality type researchers have noticed that Type C personality "is [more likely to be] a consumer of a diet high in sugar, high in saturated/trans-fats, and high in processed and refined foods." They're emotional eaters because they're emotionally corrupt. More of Mate's observations:

> *Emotional expression, in Mate's view is absolutely essential because feelings serve to alert the individual to what is dangerous or unwholesome–or, conversely, to what is helpful and nourishing–so that the person can either take protective action against the thread or move toward the beneficial stimulus.* If someone never gets angry, this reflects an unhealthy inability or unwillingness to **defend personal integrity.** *Such "boundary confusion" can ultimately become a matter of life and death. If someone just cannot say no, Mate argues, his or her body will end up saying it in the form of illness or disease.*

Put simply, nice people are fuck ups and their diets are fucked up.

CHAPTER 10 THE ALIVE JUICE BAR DIET

Here's how people are fucking things up in their own fucked up way: having *dessert for breakfast.*

Examples:

*Muffin and coffee

*Sugary cereal w/milk and orange juice

* Donut and coffee

* Pancakes or waffles w/syrup, orange juice, coffee, and bacon

All of the above are desserts. And that's what most Americans are having for breakfast. When you have dessert for breakfast, you become emotionally unstable. When you're emotionally unstable, you crave comfort — from sugar to heroin to alcohol — anything to alleviate the pain and anxiety. Some person once said:

Rob Faigin *and others have postulated that having obscene amounts of sugar and carbohydrate over long periods of time can max out our serotonin machinery, leaving us unhappy, carb-craving, and depressed.*

Another person said something similar to above:

Serotonin acts as a neurotransmitter, relaying signals from one area of the brain to another. Researchers believe that an imbalance in serotonin levels can cause depression, obsessive-compulsive disorder, panic anxiety disorder and anger management issues.

And scientists at Bartles and James University fed one group of lab mice salads and another group of lab mice muffins and found that

...the mice who ate salad for a month were able to run on wheel 74 percent longer than the muffin group. These mice also produced 84 percent more offspring. They also smiled **58 percent more often, and were 77 percent less likely to strangle another.**

Point is, having dessert for breakfast will make you batshit crazy. So don't do it. Yet people will continue to do it — especially if getting up sucks — because it's like heroin. It's a psychological pain killer.

> They eat veggies. That's why they're happy.

Breakfast That Won't Make You Batshit Crazy

Someone once wrote:

> ...a new study from scientists in England and Australia finds that simply eating more fruit and vegetables can dramatically improve your level of happiness. The researchers claim the effect is so powerful that people who went from eating zero servings of fruit and vegetables a day to eight servings per day experienced an increase in happiness and satisfaction "equivalent to moving from unemployment to employment."

So why not have salad and a protein (like an egg) for breakfast? Here's a protein shake recipe:

*avocado (as thickener)

* random veggies (broccoli, asparagus, cauliflower, whatever)

* almond or soy milk (any liquid as long as it's not fruit juice)

* random fruit (if you prefer sweeter version)

* protein powder

* adjust ratios based on taste and texture preferences

That's a nutritionally complete breakfast. It has enough fat (from avocado), protein, and a lot of fiber. And the nutrients to keep you happy and healthy instead of crashing after a couple of hours. If you don't like protein powder, pair the salad with an egg or chicken soup — whatever, as long as you're getting protein. It's important to pair the salad with a protein.

She doesn't eat veggies. And she had a donut for breakfast. That's why her cat took a shit in her shoes.

The Alive Juice Bar Diet: Start and End With Salad

Meal 1: Salad + Protein.

Meal 2: Whatever you want.

Meal 3: Whatever you want.

Meal 4: Salad (can be merged with Meal 3)

Whatever you want for the Second Meal because I'm betting that you'll be able to self-regulate if you start your day with a salad. You won't be an emotional mess when you eat that second meal so you'll exercise better judgment and control. You'll also feel full faster because you're not nutritionally depleted and therefore eat less.

Or think of Second Meal as a reward for starting your morning right.

Try it. If you don't feel better after a month, we'll give you a $100 gift card.

They're eating veggies. That's why they're not batshit crazy.

CHAPTER 11 WHY PEOPLE HATE MCDONALD'S

Would you work for a Fortune 500 company with the following profile:

* Has an African-American CEO

* Honored by Black Enterprise as one of the best companies for diversity at staff and corporate levels

* Provides all expense paid college credit eligible education at its business management school.

* Promotes from within and doesn't discriminate against those without college degrees when hiring for executive level positions, including CEO.

* Invests in progressive businesses — ie. Chipotle — that raise the standard of fast-food and build green storefronts

Who that? You know the answer, title gives it away: McDonald's. If you feel thrown off, then we're ready to begin.

ANDREW AN AN HO

Why People Hate McDonald's

Top 5 reasons — qualitatively gathered — in no particular order:

1. They treat their employees like shit.

2. Their food tastes like shit.

3. They put shit in their food.

4. Their food makes people look like shit.

5. They use manipulative advertising to get kids addicted to eating shit.

All of which need to be translated, those are just codes meant to deflect attention. There's something else going on here. Not just projection, there's sublimation, that "mature" defense mechanism, says Freud: when you replace urge to do something that *you* think is socially unacceptable with socially acceptable stand-in. Like Luke becoming an NFL linebacker so he doesn't end up in jail for beating the shit out of that motherfucker. Jenna marrying ultra-stylish Jack the hairdresser to keep Dad proud. Sam becoming a proctologist because he was raised Catholic strict.

Top 5 Reasons to Hate McDonald's, Deconstructed and Debunked

They treat their employees like shit

Pay for non-managerial staff is comparable to what a typical hospital pays its resident MDs; similar to what the university pays its graduate student TAs and RAs; almost as much as what a community college pays its adjunct professors to teach. (I could go on). Yet people aren't boycotting their hospitals and schools due to employee pay and career growth opportunities.

In providing career growth opportunities, McDonald's has most businesses — Alive Juice Bar included — beat: you can be of humble origins and degree-less and still become its CEO, as Charlie Bell (who started working at McDonald's at 15) had. Free education for its management trainees. One of few businesses willing to give those with no experience and skills (and the wrong color) a chance.

Their food tastes like shit.

It's how you frame and present something. *Watch this prank:*

Summary for those who can't watch it: pranksters pose as chefs of high end restaurant. They serve samples of their food — McDonald's fare, actually — at food expo. Some who sample rave about taste and high quality of food:

The 'Chicken McNuggets' were neatly cut up and served by a charming young waiter, complete with tidy uniform. "Rolls around the tongue nicely, if it were wine I'd say it's fine," *an older and presumably more experienced food critic commented.*

"The structure is good, yes. Not too sticky," *said one expert about a McMuffin. Then it was onto the 'real classics'.*

"You can just tell this is a lot more pure," *came another comment from a young lady operating an organic stall.*

It's like those studies that show a painting of, say, a boy pissing on a tree. Take that painting, make two of them, date one at 1500, another at present day and attribute it to someone who doesn't look like a painter. Most will describe the first as some Renaissance classic. The latter as ghetto trash. Which is it?

Renaissance era painting or two boys tugging on each others' penis. A classic or kiddie porn?

Point is, we're tools. We're not trained to think or to ask questions, we're trained to respond on cue, like caged rats in an experiment:

Organic........Fresh

Gluten-free......Healthy

Grass-fed.......Tasty

Fat-free.........Healthy

Wild...........Fresh

Even though organic has nothing to do with freshness, gluten-free isn't healthier if you're not celiac, and grass-fed isn't necessarily tastier, you get the idea. Our brains exaggerate and mix and match correlations.

They put shit in their food.

A few examples:

Earthworms (1978)

Mutant Lab Meat (2000)

Cow Eyeballs (2006)

Random Rot Preventing Chemicals (200?)

Blood libel, definition (Wiki): "accusation that Jews kidnapped and murdered children of Christians to use their blood as part of their religious rituals during Jewish holidays." The world may change, but human nature remains the same: we're still mean-spirited and vindictive. About what, we'll get to later.

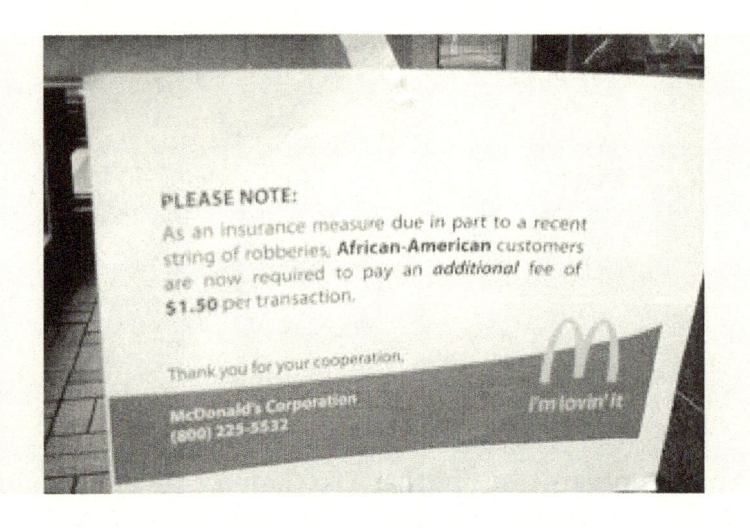

Who is more dangerous, the person who created this hoax, or those who believe it?

Their food makes people look like shit.

You can do a lot worse at a neighborhood Greek diner or Chinese take-out or Tacqueria, where portion sizes and calorie counts are even more ridiculous. Or at a fine-dining steakhouse like Metropolitan Grill or El Gaucho — 3,000 calories easy for someone who orders 1 entree, 1 salad, 1 drink, and a desert. Grande Frappuccino plus blueberry muffin at Starbucks is 700 nutritionally deficient calories. Not saying McDonald's Value Meals provide the balanced and diverse nutrition we try to get customers to consistently eat, they don't. I'm just wondering why McDonald's gets blamed for the obesity epidemic when they don't serve anywhere near the most nutritionally appalling meals.

They use manipulative advertising to get kids addicted to eating shit.

Anthony Bourdain describes McDonald's advertising tactics as "Black Propaganda." (He exaggerates, but let's work with it). And so? Try to think of an (effective) ad that isn't manipulative, that provides a cold, detached, balanced review of a product's benefits and a brand's purpose. Is there a nation that doesn't use propaganda to control its populace? Find me a person who isn't manipulative and I'll stop charging customers $1 for Better Service.

How to Figure People Out

Asking what someone likes doesn't reveal much about the person.

"The woman I like is smart, sexy, confident, tomboy by day, sex kitten by night, looks good in either jeans or a dress..." which reveals that this guy is a fucking tool, a dull one at that. A better way to figure out who someone is — personality and social status — and how they'll act is to mix it up and ask what they dislike. Here's a real life example, from an interview with an applicant:

Interviewer: *What are your career goals?*

Applicant: *I hope to work at Woman, Infants, and Children (WIC) food stamps program. I want to help the poor make better choices with their food stamp money. I want to help the poor eat better.*

Interviewer: *What do you think about Roger's Market? (Roger's is an independent grocery store in Mountlake Terrace, primarily serving low income residents. Lots of food stamps).*

Applicant*: It's disgusting, everything about it. I try to stay away from there.*

Interviewer*: Then you won't last 2 weeks working at the WIC.*

Applicant: *Huh?*

Interviewer*: You just told me you hate poor people. If you can't stand shopping at Roger's, where those with food stamps shop, then how are you going to work with them on a near daily basis?*

Not saying she's insincere about her desire to help the poor eat better. Just saying this desire is driven by a conflict within herself she doesn't understand and doesn't want to acknowledge because it's too painful to do so. When we cross-check this interview transcript with applicant resume and Facebook page, what emerges is a standard lower middle-class female who's one wrong move from becoming White trash. That's why she spends money she doesn't have on microbrews and listens to college radio. That's why she goes into debt to get a bullshit degree at a bullshit college, to gain some psychological (but ephemeral) distance from the wrong side of the tracks, even at the risk of having the debt force her to stand in line for food stamps. And it's precisely that risk — unacknowledged but instinctively recognized — that makes her hate those she's afraid of becoming. That's why she expresses her repressed hatred by seeking a career that allows her to "help" those she hates, that confirms her identity as not one of them.

Why We Actually Don't Hate McDonald's

Hating McDonald's is like hating your great-grandmother for being a racist. She's an icon for lasting this long, so you forgive her faults. McDonald's is an American icon, and they know it, which is why they're using sentimental ads to make you less pissed off at them, to remind you of a time when everyone, regardless of social class and race, ate at McDonald's without guilt.

Thesis: those who hate McDonald's don't hate McDonald's. They hate McDonald's customers. They hate the stereotype of those who regularly eat at McDonald's. They hate poor people, and the ones afraid that they themselves will end up poor probably hate themselves too. Let's return to the 5 reasons why people hate McDonald's.

1. They treat their employees like shit.

2. Their food tastes like shit.

3. They put shit in their food.

4. Their food makes people look like shit.

5. They use manipulative advertising to get kids addicted to eating shit.

Above 5 is how we routinely describe the poor. It's the poor, the thinking goes, who get paid and treated like shit. It's the poor who eat food that tastes like shit; who are pathetic enough to eat food that literally is shit; who are obese; who are stupid enough to be so easily manipulated.

But we've been taught that it's socially unacceptable to shit on the poor. So we displace our hate onto the biggest piece of cultural flotsam we see, the number one fast food company in the world. Calling out the Greek diner or Chinese takeout or the dive bar that serves too much alcohol is too politically problematic — these are hard working immigrants making a living by providing what people want and blaming alcohol will lead to riots. But blaming a giant corporation for serving what people want *is* socially acceptable, a lot more so than telling your daughter to lose 50 pounds.

It's easier to blame McDonald's for making people fat than to blame fat people for making themselves fat, *possibly* from eating at McDonald's. It's more comforting: "It's not my fault my kids are obese," rationalizes Mom's defense mechanism. "If we just get rid of fast food and raise wages, these people wouldn't act as they do," the Champagne Socialist who has never lived among non-immigrant American poor surmises. In other words, it's more comforting to believe that we don't control our destiny, that virtue and character don't emerge from that struggle within, that it's simply a matter of public fucking policy. Fix the policy and we'll have Heaven on Earth, the thinking goes, as people wait and wait and wait for the government to get it right.

The problem isn't McDonald's. McDonald's is just providing what some people want and making McDonald's disappear isn't going to make a difference — none at all — because people will get what they want and what they deserve, regardless of public policy and intervening laws. The problem is us. We're the ones who are suspicious instead of skeptical, gullible instead of judicious, and fearful of our place in a rapidly changing society.

Nietzsche on the Monsters we fight (from Beyond Good and

Evil):

"Those who fight Monsters should look to it that they themselves do not become Monsters. And when you gaze long into the Abyss, the Abyss also gazes into you."

And the only experience more terrifying than the abyss gazing back into you is when it offers you a Big Mac and Fries, which you then eat alone.

CHAPTER 12 SOY, MEN, AND TITTIES

Some guys are refusing soy milk because they've heard that consuming soy promotes growth of women style breasts in men. I call bullshit.

Here's what WebMD has to say about soy: **Four Soy Food Myths Exposed**

Summary: soy is a good and complete source of protein. It doesn't cause cancer and it won't turn men with gender identity anxiety issues into this:

Transgendered

What ZocDoc blog has to say about soy and man boobs: **Does Soy "Feminize" Men? Fact Vs. Myth**

Summary: Soy does not turn a guy into anything close to a woman unless — maybe — you drink like three quarts of it per day. Which you probably won't, even Asians don't come close to consuming that amount. Author's recommendation:

If you're a man and trying to avoid even small amounts of something that may lead to breast development, that's probably not the right approach. There are benefits of soy that may make regular consumption worthwhile, such as its role in protecting against prostate cancer. Remember, it's the dose that makes the poison.

And look at Asian men. There are, like what, half a billion Asians who eat soy everyday. Asians have been eating soy daily for centuries. Say what you want about small dicks and smooth bodies, but when is the last time you saw an Asian guy — ladyboy Thai guys don't count, those are implants — with titties? More proof:

ANDREW AN AN HO

No titties

HOW TO EAT LIKE AN ASSHOLE

He drinks soy milk everyday. No titties.

ANDREW AN AN HO

He eats stinky tofu everyday. For past 10 years. Still no titties

HOW TO EAT LIKE AN ASSHOLE

His Mom forced him to eat edamame everyday. No titties.

ANDREW AN AN HO

Those are not titties, those are fat man boobs. He got those from eating too many fries and drinking too much soda and jerking off everyday to Asian porn. Not from eating soy.

They say J Crispy Dickhead has titties. Not sure, hard to tell with shirt on. J Crispy Dickhead does not eat soy.

CHAPTER 13 HOW TO GET KIDS TO EAT THEIR VEGGIES AND TO LOVE THEIR PARENTS

Let's back up so we can get to the source of the problem. How do you get someone to fall in love with you? Pick:

a) Be really really nice to that person.

b) Hire a witch, cast a love spell.

c) Get that person to do things for you.

Option A doesn't work, it gets you either ignored or used because nice is cheap, it's ineffective, it's too easy to pull off, there's too much of it around.

Option B comes with a lot of side-effects and it can get weird when the spell hits the wrong target so better not.

Option C works, not because "relationship experts" say so, but because it's the option that requires the most work. Life isn't supposed to be easy.

Why Kids Don't Love Their Parents

People assume their kids love them because they think it's a law of nature for kids to love their parents. Not so, according to the Story of Oedipus, that motherfucker murdered his dad and then fucked his mom. This story endures in public consciousness because it reminds us of the uncomfortable truths we'd prefer to not think about, or to only consider academically. Deep down, and in spite of incessant bromides about self-love as the solution, we know we're no longer in the Garden of Eden and we're unsure of what to do about it.

What makes the Story of Oedipus so unsettling and compelling is that while every character in the story knew what was *supposed* to go down, *nobody knew what was happening.* That's the most terrifying kind of horror. If it had just been a story about some kid throwing a shit fit for getting grounded and killing dad and raping mom in the process, we'd treat it as a sad and tragic spectacle and assume the kid became a sociopath because he was molested by his football coach and his mom was a drunk who called him a "stupid, useless, cunt" one too many times.

Instead, it's a story about funked up shit happening to good people who try their best as parents. Oedipus was born to good parents who had to make a difficult decision — abort their only child to save the kingdom and themselves. So they left him for dead in the middle of nowhere. Oedipus, luckily (or unluckily), was found and saved by someone and then adopted by good parents — king and queen from another kingdom. And he tried to be a good son — when a prophet told him that he'd kill his dad and fuck his mom, he exiled himself, not realizing that he would soon unknowingly encounter his birth dad.

Only encounter with birth dad, they squabble and Oedipus beats the shit out of him, killing him. First prophesy fulfilled and nobody realizes it. Which invites us to ask unsettling questions about ourselves: would I love my parents/children if they weren't my parents/children? Would I hate them and want to kill them, as Oedipus did? Would my kid love me if she didn't need me to survive?

How many of us are Oedipus? How many of us don't want to kill dad and rape mom, but do so anyway, *without realizing it*?

How to Teach Kids to Love Their Parents

The Story of Oedipus reminds us that we live in a cruel and lonely world and nothing should be taken for granted. We can't assume there's an unbreakable and spiritual love-bond between a parent and a child. And whatever bond there is is sociological and ephemeral, love requires a lot of work and perseverance. Check out the confessions section of **Scary Mommy** website if you don't believe me.

If love is an action and not a feeling, then like most actions, it has to be taught and practiced, it doesn't just happen. Teaching a kid to love a parent requires the same effort as making friends or getting someone to fall in love with you, it's the same dynamic. To make friends, you have to figure out a way to get that person to do something for you so they become emotionally invested in you. Benjamin Franklin, from his autobiography, on how to make friends:

He that has once done you a kindness will be more ready to do you *another, than he whom you yourself have obliged.[*

Make the person do something for you. Make them *invest in you*. Below is an example of how Franklin turned an enemy into a friend:

Having heard that he had in his library a certain very scarce and curious book, I wrote a note to him, expressing my desire of perusing that book, and requesting he would do me the favour of lending it to me for a few days. He sent it immediately, and I return'd it in about a week with another note, expressing strongly my sense of the favour. When we next met in the House, he spoke to me (which he had never done before), and with great civility; and he ever after manifested a readiness to serve me on all occasions, so that we became great friends, and our friendship continued to his death.

Take something away from someone if you want to make an enemy. Give something away for free too often if you want to be used and disrespected. Have someone give you something if you want a friend. Same dynamic when seeking romantic love, according to random "romantic relationship expert":

In fact, when people see you doing stuff for them for free, unsolicited, or uncompensated, their thought is never, "Wow, what a great guy! I should repay him in spades!" but rather, "Oh, that's nice – it's nice having nice people around like this who give me stuff. Thanks, nice person!"

Yeah yeah, I know your friend paid you back with food and drink when you helped her move. That's why you're friends. You wouldn't be friends anymore if she hadn't reciprocated, right? Because it'd be *disrespectful* to not reciprocate. Yet there are parents who keep giving and giving and giving to their kids while getting little or nothing in return; or the nice guy who keeps paying for dates and buying gifts but can't get a commitment or even a make out session from his crush. Parents will then blame technology and culture for producing entitled, disrespectful and narcissistic kids; the nice guy will blame women for preferring assholes. Both of which are lame excuses that prevents them from blaming the source of the problem: themselves.

Nice people are liked, but not respected, we learn from history and classical literature and political philosophy. "Now that's fucked up," some of you are thinking, "I won't play that game." Fine, but don't play martyr when disrespected because it's a lot easier to play Santa than to empower someone to become whom she wants to be. Kobe Bryant, one of the most disliked AND respected NBA players of all-time on what he wished he had done with his money when he made his first millions early in his career:

You will come to understand that you were taking care of them because it made YOU feel good; it made YOU happy to see them smiling and without a care in the world...While you were feeling satisfied with yourself, you were slowly eating away at their own dreams and ambitions. You were adding material things to their lives, but subtracting the most precious gifts of all: independence and growth.

"While you were feeling satisfied with yourself," because Kobe's been there, he's done that. He knows a handout is the quintessential narcissistic douche bag act that's neither effective nor an act of love precisely because it's the easy thing to do to gain short-term pleasure at the expense of another person's dignity and long-term happiness. Kobe on how he wished he had treated people when he earned his first millions:

When your [NBA] dream comes true...you need to figure out a way to invest in the future of your family and friends. "I said INVEST. I did not say GIVE.

Invest means not giving girlfriend the weekend getaway she wants until she passes a section of the CPA exam she's been studying for; no blowjobs until husband sets personal sales record for the month; no squeaky toy for dog until she learns a new obstacle course; no catnip until the cat catches that mouse. This is how people and animals learn to perform at high levels. And that's why it's so hard to do so, why it's easier to give than to invest: investing requires self-denial, patience, respect, and the ability to enter another's spirit. Giving merely fulfills immediate needs, it's like giving heroin to someone who is in pain, or candy to a kid so he stops crying. Kobe on the effectiveness of investing rather than giving:

As time goes on, you will see them grow independently and have their own ambitions and their own lives, and your relationship with all of them will be much better as a result.

So how do we *teach* a kid to love his parents? To begin with, teach the kid to become *emotionally invested* in the parents. And it starts early, by drilling habits. Meaning, parents don't tie a kid's shoes, kid ties parents's shoes and shines them. Parents don't spend money to entertain kids, kids entertain parents by memorizing and reciting parent's favorite poems and performing their favorite songs. Parents don't pay for a kid's pedicure and massage session just because, kid massages her parents feet every day after school to earn that right once a quarter. Parents don't cook and clean for kids, kid cooks and clean for parents and if the food sucks, send it back, have kid redo it because that's how it is in the real world. Parents don't take their kid out to dinner to celebrate their first job; kid takes parents out to dinner when he gets his first paycheck to thank them for the opportunity to have a job and for driving him to and from. Parents don't pay for kid's grand tour after college graduation, kid saves and saves and saves to send parents on all-expense paid vacation to thank them. Parents don't buy their kids their first house, kids buy parents a vacation home before buying their first. That's how to teach a kid to not send parents to a decrepit rat-infested nursing home when the parent turns geriatric. That's how to teach a kid that love is an act, not a narcissistic and impressionistic feeling.

"But they won't do any of the above," some parents are thinking. Then reject them, just as you should reject an abusive spouse or a friend who stabs you in the back. Because when a kid takes and takes and takes and never gives only asks for more, that's abuse, they're learning how to be abusive and they're going to be abusers as adults. Why put up with it? Why feed it? Only people who suffer from Battered Spouse Syndrome put up with that kind of shit.

HOW TO EAT LIKE AN ASSHOLE

She knows, because she forgave him after she caught him fucking her sister.

Battered Woman Syndrome

Unmet needs/Unresolved issues → Anxiety, insecurity, depression → Seeking love as a solution → Finding temporary relief → Pleasing and appeasing your partner → Partner is controlling and abusive → You're angry, afraid and/or withdrawn → He and/or you seek reconciliation → Things get "back to normal"

She gives all her money to her daughter. Her daughter routinely calls her a "cunt" and tells her to "shut the fuck up" when asked to do the dishes.

How to Get Kid Who Doesn't Want to Eat Veggies to Eat Them

Answer is the same as how to get a kid to love their parents. Back to the question asked in the beginning:

How do you get someone to fall in love with you? (Or, how do you get your kid to love you)? Correct answer in bold:

a) Be really really nice to that person.

b) Hire a witch, cast a love spell.

c) Get that person to do things for you

Which is easier said than done. It takes a lot of work to get a kid to be emotionally invested in their parents' well being by teaching and training her to take care of her parents the moment she can walk on her own. If she doesn't get in the habit of doing things for her parents early in her life, she won't do it when parents are late in their lives. Amy Chua (aka Tiger Cunt to some) knows that so she trains her daughters — even at ages 20 and 23 — to be her bitches. Here's a contract she wrote and had them sign when she sensed her daughters were going to take advantage of her generosity:

*WHEREAS **Amy Chua** and Jed Rubenfeld are the owners of Apt. [XXX] at [XXX], and their children are not;*

WHEREAS Children owe their parents everything, even in the West, where many have conflicted feelings about this;

NOW THEREFORE

In exchange for Amy and Jed allowing them to stay in their NYC apartment from June 1, 2016 to August 1, 2016, Sophia Chua-Rubenfeld and Louisa Chua-Rubenfeld agree to the following irrevocable duties and conditions:

1. To occupy only the junior bedroom.

2. To greet Jed Rubenfeld & Amy Chua with spontaneous joy and gratitude whenever they visit.

3. To make their (joint) bed every day, and not to fight about who does it.

4. To never, ever use the phrase, "Relax—it's not a big deal."

5. To always leave all internal doors in the apartment wide open whenever Jed, Amy or any company whatsoever (including relatives) are in the apartment, with an immaculately made bed in full view and no clothing or other junk on the floor of the bedroom in sight.

6. Whenever any guests visit, to come out of the bedroom immediately in a respectable state, greet the guests with enthusiasm, and sit and converse with the guests in the living room for at least 15 minutes.

7. To always be kind to our trusty Samoyeds Coco and Pushkin, who Sophia and Louisa hereby agree have greater rights to the apartment than Sophia and Louisa do, and to walk them to the dog park at least once a day when they visit, within 30 minutes of being asked to do so by Amy.

8. To fill the refrigerator with fresh OJ from Fairway for Jed on days when he is in town.

9. To keep the pillows in the living room in the right place and PLUMPED and to clean the glass table with Windex whenever it is used.

ADDITIONALLY, Sophia and Louisa agree that the above duties and conditions will not be excused even in the event of illness, hangovers, migraines, work crises or mental breakdowns (whether their own or their friends').

Sophia and Louisa agree that if they violate any one of these conditions, Amy and Jed will have the right to get the Superintendent or a doorman to restrain them from entering the apartment; and to change the locks.

All of which are reasonable requests since they're getting free rent in one of the most expensive real estate markets in the world. Tiger Cunt on above contract:

The fact is, we're never off the hook as parents. Even when your kids are in their 20s, it's still a constant balancing act. Are we asking too much of them or too little? Are we being strong and holding them to a high standard, or just being too critical? Are we teaching them by example how to live a happy, meaningful, giving life?

More importantly, she's teaching them how to reciprocate and to not take advantage of other people's kindness. She's teaching them how to be gracious. She's teaching them how to love. She doesn't hope for reciprocity and respect, she demands it.

From UK Guardian:

Food researchers at Ohio State University and Cornell University in New York found that children are five times more likely to eat salad when they have grown it themselves.

Children who are *emotionally invested* in the food in front of them are more likely to eat it. They don't necessarily have to grow it — they can prep or serve it, for instance — they just have to be involved in the work of making a meal happen to become emotionally invested.

HOW TO EAT LIKE AN ASSHOLE

Her smile isn't fake, she wasn't forced to smile. She grows and eats her veggies.

Third graders in Japan serving food to classmates. Even though they're not smiling, they're still happy. Or maybe they're not happy about having to drink milk because they're lactose intolerant, as are most Asians. Either way, they're going to eat their veggies. Unless the Washington Post reporter is lying. If he is, he's a dickhead.

How to Get Kids Involved in Making Their Own Meals

But some kids don't want to be involved in making their own meals. Which brings us back to the source of the problem: *kids who've never been trained to love their parents* (don't misread that, read it carefully). That's where it begins. A lot of people think that pain-in-the-ass kids are the way they are because their parents haven't loved them enough, haven't done enough for them. No, look around, look especially at the middle-class fuck ups, they're the way they are not because they grew up poor or their parents have neglected them or they weren't loved enough, but because *they've never had to do anything for their parents. They never had to earn their parent's love. They never learned to love.*

A child who doesn't know how to love another isn't going to be able to learn how to love eating veggies. Such a child is accustomed to receiving love (pleasure) from his parents without having to work for it. So why would he want to work at improving his palate when he's been trained to receive pleasure immediately and often, without pain and effort? Getting such a child to eat vegetables is the least of our worries. There's going to be meth addiction.

Love isn't the solution, it should be the end result. By making love the solution, it becomes the problem. Children don't need more love, they need to learn how to love. Only when they learn to love will they be ready to experience how good a succulent bite of sausage can be when preceded with a crisp bite of lightly sauteed zucchini; and appreciate the effort put into loving them from those who love them the most.

CHAPTER 14 DO YOU HAVE FEELINGS ABOUT FEELINGS?

If you do, then you're batshit crazy. I'll explain.

How American Culture Makes People Batshit Crazy

The most disturbing aspect — the source of all these mental and dietary health problems in the US — about American culture (Anglo culture, really) is that it trains people to have feelings about feelings. Like Chelsea getting mad at herself for being mad at her boyfriend because his wee wee malfunctioned at the wrong time; Jessica feeling guilty about being happy after she beats her bestie to win State. Robbie getting depressed because he's not who he thought he was now that he's harboring racist thoughts after getting carjacked twice in two months by Black dudes; Susan afraid about becoming anxious during her solo.

What happens above is learned — vis-a-vis American moral education — and it's not natural or healthy to behave like that. Real, raw, instinctive emotions are already tough enough to deal with, adding a layer of manufactured ones is bound to drive people nuts not just because there are more emotions to deal with, but because now there are conflicting emotions that make people's internal compass — ie. instincts — go haywire. Without instincts, people are as good as dead.

Below are some emotions Americans are taught to avoid feeling

- Anger
- Hate
- Fear
- Sadness
- Anxiety

because they're "negative." Okay, how so? Dylan Thomas didn't think anger a negative emotion when he wrote to his dying father:

And you, my father, there on the sad height,

Curse, bless me now with your fierce tears, I pray.

Do not go gentle into that good night.

Rage, rage against the dying of the light.

Or how about Jesus Christ, who goes ape shit on those who fuck with his shit? From the book of Matthew 21:12-13:

12 And Jesus entered the temple[a] and drove out all who sold and bought in the temple, and he overturned the tables of the money-changers and the seats of those who sold pigeons. 13 He said to them, "It is written, 'My house shall be called a house of prayer,' but you make it a den of robbers."

Don't piss off Jesus. Or he'll go ape shit on you.

What about fear? Courage isn't the absence of fear, it's the ability to move forward despite fear. If there's no fear, there's no courage and courage is one of those acts that make life worth living. Beginning to see how those who run away from so called negative emotions are spiritually dead? It's the combination of anger and fear that makes courage possible. Passion is the combination of anger and love. Fear and anxiety (or as Kierkegaard puts it, "Fear and Trembling") makes faith. Now imagine life without courage, passion, and faith. Is it worth living?

Yet the curators of American culture insist that courage is possible only when there's no fear, serenity if there's no anger, success if there's no anxiety, love if there's no hate, happiness if there's no sadness, pleasure if there's no pain. As with all attempts to create Heaven on Earth, the unintended consequences have been disastrous: more emotional eating, more drug addiction, more mental health problems.

How People are Trained to Have Feelings About Feelings, (how to become emotionally corrupt)

Again, it's not natural to have feelings about feelings (aka meta-feelings). Real emotions are instinctual and their purpose is to protect the feeler of them: fear when you unexpectedly encounter a lion in the wild; sadness when your beloved child dies; anger when cheated by a trusted friend; happiness when your team wins. Fake emotions, on the other hand — and this includes sentimentality, that "failure of feeling" and "mask of cruelty" — are taught. Here's how:

Parent says: Don't be mad at me!

Kid hears: It's wrong to be angry

Teacher says: Don't be sad!

Kid hears: There's something wrong with feeling sad.

Coach says: Don't be nervous!

Kid hears: There's something wrong with feeling anxious

Commercial says: Don't be scared!

Kid hears: There's something wrong with feeling scared.

Customer says: You need to smile more if you want a tip (some cunt actually said this at another juice bar)

Employee hears: I need to be happy all the time for people to like me

Stranger says: I'm fine, how are you?

You hear: Everyone is always happy, why not me?

How do you think those bombarded with these asinine messages and exhortations are going to turn out? Erika the waitress is going to get stoned every day before work so she looks happy, dopey, and smiley for the pleasure of her emotionally corrupt customers who think going to a restaurant should be the same experience as going to Disneyland. Jane, who once practiced and practiced to become a concert pianist now needs anxiety meds to make it to school, much less to Carnegie Hall. Adam becomes a heroin addict because he lacks the anger to produce the natural pain-killers that'd get him through work drug free. Emily is on depression meds and when she's not she binges on carbs because that's what happens when you're scared of being sad.

Bloody British Cunts   (aka BBC)

In 2017, the BBC ran a health story titled "Anger and hatred can make us feel happy, study says." This cross-cultural study "included some 2,300 university students from the United States, Brazil, China, Germany, Ghana, Israel, Poland and Singapore." One conclusion:

People are happier if they are able to feel emotions they desire – even if those emotions are unpleasant, such as anger and hatred."

Specific emotions don't make people happy. It's the ability to feel what one wants to feel that makes one happy. Put differently elsewhere in the article:

The researchers found that while people overall wanted to experience more pleasant emotions, they had the greatest life satisfaction if the emotions they experienced matched those they desired.

Another conclusion, that Westerners are unhappy because they're hedonistic:

People want to feel very good all the time in Western cultures. Even if they feel good most of the time, they may still think that they should feel even better, which might make them less happy overall.

Since the BBC is run by a bunch of Bloody British Cunts, this article is biased as fuck: it assigns Anglo-centric moral value to specific emotions. Anger and hate, for instance, are described as "unpleasant" and "negative" emotions. Except they're not but by cultural decree. Which emotion do professional athletes use most often to stay focused and to play through pain: happiness or anger? Anger, of course, because that's the emotion that releases natural pain killers in our bodies and improves focus and strength. I may be despicable and an angry motherfucker, but there isn't one customer who'd describe me as lacking in motivation and vigor precisely because I allow myself to access the full spectrum of emotions — without judgment — and anyone who tells me how I ought to feel can kiss my ass.

Grandpa Hates Japs

My Chinese aunt once paid a compliment to the Japanese. Since her father (my grandfather) was present, she prefaced it with:

I hate the Japanese as much as anyone, but I have to admire how they've...

The preface makes clear that there's no taboo among the Chinese against hating an ethnic group. In this case, this show of (manufactured) hate is used positively, as a show of respect for an elder's experiences and perspective. Nobody in the family calls grandpa a racist for hating the Japanese, nobody tries to change his mind. I mean, why shouldn't he hate the Japanese — he grew up watching them rape and pillage half his fucking country. Not saying forgiveness isn't a better option, but that's for him to decide, not anyone else, because none of us understand what he experienced so it's best to leave him be. He'll stop hating once he's ready to do so, not when other people tell him to do so.

Photos of beheaded civilians from Rape of Nanking. How soon would you hate and how long would it take you to forgive?

Stand-Up Comedy Doesn't Exist in China (and what that has to do with the cost of therapy)

Nor in Russia, Germany, France, most of the world actually. Stand-up comedy is a uniquely Anglo invention, started and gained popularity in the UK during the emotionally repressive and imperialistically expansive Victorian Era (1837-1901). Historian Harold Perkins writes about the transformation of manners during the time leading into the Victorian Era:

Between 1780 and 1850 the English ceased to be one of the most aggressive, brutal, rowdy, outspoken, riotous, cruel and bloodthirsty nations in the world and became one of the most inhibited, polite, orderly, tender-minded, prudish and hypocritical.

In other words, Anglos went from being assholes to being politically correct, self-righteous, emotionally timid, phlegmatic assholes. Why did this transformation of manners happen? Let's see what was happening geopolitically. During the 19th century, the British Empire added

...around 10,000,000 square miles (26,000,000 km2) of territory and roughly 400 million people were added to the British Empire. Unchallenged at sea, Britain adopted the role of global policeman... Alongside the formal control it exerted over its own colonies, Britain's dominant position in world trade meant that it effectively controlled the economies of many countries, such as China, Argentina, and Siam, which has been described by some historians as an Informal Empire. (wiki entry on British Empire).

Here are a few details about what the British were up to:

- 1789 To annihilate Australian aboriginals, British military brought bottles of smallpox to infect them. Ninety percent of aboriginal population died within 15 months.
- 1806 Abandonment of Spanish POWs on barren island on the Rio de la Plata river during Napoleonic Wars to starve to death.

- 1842 To reverse trade imbalance, Britain forces China to legalize and buy its opium, leading to an opioid epidemic that nearly destroys China.
- 1845-1849 British policies lead to the Great Potato Famine in Ireland, resulting in one million dead and another million emigrating to escape starvation because throughout the famine, the British continued to export out of Ireland agricultural products, such as wheat and beef, the English wanted.
- 1857 The aftermath of the Indian Rebellion (1857–58), when convicted mutineers were tied in front of cannons and blasted, or sewn into pig or cow skins after death (for Muslims and Hindus respectively).
- 1899-1902 The roundup of Boer civilians (mostly women and children) into the world's first modern "concentration camps" during the Second Boer War

Is it an accident that the rapid rise of Britain to world dominance coincides with the sudden transformation of Anglo manners? I doubt it. To begin with, what do the British need to do to convince their subjects that they deserve to be ruled by the British? What do the British need to do to convince themselves that it's their divine "burden" to rule over their colonial and neo-colonial subjects and to treat them the way they do?

Bloody British Cunts who think they're civilized even though they eat with chopsticks up their asses.

Answer: Everyone needed to be convinced that the British are more civilized, that is, more removed from the state of nature than are their subjects. And that begins with the repression of emotions and sticking a chopstick up one's ass while one eats. After all, only animals and children act on instinct, while humans act on reason only, right? Rudyard Kipling writes about the imperialist mindset, from the satirical "White Man's Burden," 1899:

Take up the White Man's burden

Send for the best ye breed

Go bind your sons to exile

To serve your captives' need;

To wait in heavy harness,

On fluttered folk and wild

Your new-caught sullen peoples,

Half-devil and half-child

British colonized these people because they squat instead of sit in chairs and eat with chopsticks instead of sticking them up their asses. Now we know that squatting is healthier than sitting. Would you prefer to be "civilized" or healthy?

Anglo politeness, especially in the US, has become like religious prayers, entreaties for forgiveness for the forgotten and denied sins of a nation and its individual citizens. Americans will, for instance, incessantly and inappropriately say "please" and "thank you," as if chanting a mantra to showcase their good breeding and virtuous intentions, when in fact, these gratuitous mutterings are meant to mask their bigotry, hypocrisy, and cruelty. The more vile and socially inept they are, the more polite they are.

Which brings us back to the question: "Why is stand-up comedy a uniquely Anglo form of entertainment, most popular in English speaking nations?" It doesn't exist in China or Russia or Germany, even though other forms of American and British entertainment — hip hop for instance — are popular in these nations.

Because there's no need for stand up comedy in places where political correctness doesn't exist and emotional repression isn't normal. The reason why stand-up comedy is so popular in the US is because since the end of World War II, the US has taken over the role of the world's police and asshole and now we have to convince ourselves and everyone else that we deserve that role. So we stop saying what's on our mind and feel what we want to feel in order to convince ourselves that we're somehow superior to those backward ass bigots even though we're as bigoted and hypocritical as the British at their worst. Since it's not natural and healthy to behave this way, we watch stand-up comedy to let out our repressed selves in a way that won't desecrate our carefully curated public identities — *successful stand up comedians say what everyone is thinking but are afraid to say.* Stand-up comedians are the modern court jesters of American middle-class society.

Ask a German, "How are you?" and he'll respond truthfully. Ask a Russian "How are you?" and he'll tell you it's none of your business. Ask a Chinese person that question and she'll ignore you. The people from the aforementioned don't serve customers with a smile plastered on their faces and they never, ever smile while walking down the street unless they have an instinctive reason to do so because anyone who smiles like that must either be a fraud or an idiot. They navigate with their instincts, not with what they're told is proper, polite and pleasant.

Life Doesn't Have to Be This Way

Instead of telling ourselves and each other to not be sad, or angry, or anxious...we could ask each other why we're sad, angry, or anxious, whatever it may be we're feeling. And let each other know that it's normal and expected to be anxious before performing solo, and nervous while performing it; to be angry when cheated; sad when your team loses; ashamed when you let someone down.

Instead of judging, let's ask questions. Exploring why we are who we are instead of hiding who we are may be the first step toward recovery from an addiction to overthinking that's ruining us.

Overthinking:
The art of creating problems that don't exist.

CHAPTER 15 HOW THE CULT OF SELF-ESTEEM PRODUCES FUCK UPS

A professional model, not quite a supermodel but aspires to become one, dumps her boyfriend. He's a good guy, has a good job, is good looking. Cock is large enough, he's just kinky enough, no premature ejack issues. Cool parents and siblings, no douchebag friends, no troubling mental health issues. Sort of a guy who gets women to battle royale each other.

Why did she dump him? Pick:

a) He criticized her looks too often.

b) He complimented her looks too often.

c) She's an arrogant, narcissistic bitch.

Think about it. We'll get back to this later. Open a bottle if you're nervous. I'm probably already ahead of you. Cheers.

Quotes From Those Most Consider Supremely Confident and Successful

Will Smith: "I still doubt myself every single day. What people believe is my self-confidence is actually my reaction to fear."

John Lennon: "Part of me suspects that I'm a loser, and the other part of me thinks I'm God Almighty."

Meryl Streep: "You think, 'Why would anyone want to see me again in a movie?' And I don't know how to act anyway, so why am I doing this?"

Maya Angelou: "I have written eleven books, but each time I think, 'Uh oh, they're going to find out now. I've run a game on everybody, and they're going to find me out.'"

"Whaaaat," some are thinking. What's with the low self-esteem? "How can...if I were..." Hold that thought. And don't project, other people are NOT you and you're not them.

Defining Self-Esteem and Self-Confidence

Don't confuse self-esteem with self-confidence, even if too many psychologists conflate the two. If you do, you won't be able to understand what's going on above. Self-esteem is one's PERCEPTION and ASSESSMENT of oneself, eg. I'm smart, I'm good looking, I'm a dumbass, I'm repulsive. Self-confidence is one's FAITH in one's ability to achieve something, eg. I'll hit 50 home runs, I can make the cover of Vogue, I can beat the shit out of that motherfucker, I'll find the cure to cancer.

Prevailing assumption is that one must have high self-esteem in order to have high self-confidence. One must think highly of oneself — "I'm brilliant! — in order to find the cure for cancer. Concomitant assumption is that those with low self-esteem will be failures and are prone to violence, drug abuse, etc. Such assumptions make it tempting to conflate self-esteem with self-confidence.

Self-esteem is rooted in one's perception of one's environment. An All-State basketball player who didn't receive D-I scholarship offers may consider himself not very good at basketball because he compares himself to D-I players. The best basketball player on a last place high school team may consider himself a great basketball player because he only compares himself to his teammates.

Self-confidence is primarily built on achievement in a competitive environment. Like the MVP of the NBA. Perfect MCAT scores. An Academy Award. The more objective the assessment of one's ability, the higher its value and impact on confidence level. (Academy Award, for instance, is partially a subjective assessment of ability).

Self-Esteem Movement

Some claim Ayn Rand's boytoy, Nathaniel Branden (of all people), started the self-esteem movement back in 1969. Whatever, who cares. Point is, the theory that one must have high self-esteem in order to have the confidence to achieve socially acceptable goals began to gain currency in academic circles sometime around that year. Theory mostly circulates in the academy for a decade, where it's refined, debated, and pushed (and tested) on eager and impressionable undergrads. Some who, ten years after graduation, began to wield socio-cultural influence, perhaps as journalists, teachers, PTA moms.

Who was listening? Champagne socialists aside, it's those who looked up to college grads. That is, those who didn't go to college but wanted so badly their kids to do so. They thought they were getting the inside scoop on how to get ahead even though it would've worked out better if son had taken over a plumbing business that pays $120,000 a year instead of getting a bullshit degree from a bullshit college. Cult of self-esteem grows as Oprah and Glamour mainstream the feel good message to the aspirational working and middle-class by growing and feeding their narcissism. Different sort of narcissism, as Machiavellianism is so passe in post-industrial America. This is narcissism by repression, projection, and ironic contradiction. Kids are taught to repress fundamental emotions such as fear and anger. Feeling hate? Project project project, "it's not me, it's him, I'm all love," rationalizes the kid robbed of his lunch money. And what better way to bolster the ego than community service? "I am special and should be admired because today, I volunteered my time to help people," she thinks as she rolls a spliff and begins four hours worth of daydreaming about her glamorous future and picking up as many "Likes" on Facebook as she needs to feel good about herself.

Tenets of Self-Esteem Movement

1. Be nice. Don't hurt anyone's feelings.

2. Focus on what one's good at instead of struggling with the unfamiliar.

3. Everyone is special, everyone's a winner

4. You can do and become whatever you want. Whatever you want (echo-o-o-o).

5. Avoid stress and pressure to maximize performance.

6. When stressed or hurt, talk about your feelings.

How the narcissist understands these tenets:

1. Don't hurt my feelings by pointing out my fuck ups. And I'll do the same for you. Deal?

2. I'm allowed to avoid reality, to not think about my fuck ups and how to fix them.

3. I should avoid situations that make me look like a loser.

4. Let me daydream and delay the inevitable realization that there are limits and achievement requires extraordinary time and effort, for which I'm not prepared.

5. Heaven on Earth is possible, the blissful life. It's ok to live life as a series of escapes.

6. It's socially acceptable to live inside one's head, and to not be responsible for one's feelings.

Self-Esteem and the Bizarre

Teen boy comes in. His parents are the types who continually remind him that "you can do whatever you want, you can be whatever you want." Places order. I begin small talk. He's a big boy so I ask: "you play football?" His response: "Nah. Football coaches think it's a waste of my physical attributes. But whatever. I can do whatever I want. I can do whatever I want."

Ok. I understand. Kumar (of Harold and Kumar) points out that just because one has a big dick doesn't mean one should become a porn star. That's fine, I get it. Then it gets weird.

"What sports do you do?"

"Track."

"Which events?"

"Pole vault."

"Aren't you kinda big for that?"

He has three options. He can tell me that I'm wrong, that he has the ideal body for such an event and explain why that's the case; or I'm right and he's an outlier. Third option is what he chose: "I can do whatever I want, man. I can do whatever I want."

Someone tell me that I'm not the only one with the urge to knock this kid out cold and lock him in a dungeon until Stockholm Syndrome sets in for life. This was a bizarre and scary exchange. Total disregard of what's best for the team. Completely focused on what the self wants. Imagine his future:

Detective: Why did you think it was ok to forcibly stick your cock in that girl's mouth?

Boy: I can do whatever I want, I can do whatever I want.

Detective: I bet you can. And Uncle Shirley can do whatever he wants, whenever he wants too. I can't wait for you to meet him.

What Kids Hear

Parent says: You can be whatever you want.

Kid hears: I will be seen as squandering my special talents and powers if I don't achieve greatness. I'm not prepared for this kind of pressure. I need to start searching for excuses.

Parent says: You can do whatever you want.

Kids hears: Who cares about the wants and needs of others.

Parent says: You did a great job, great effort kiddo.

Kids hears: Not really, but I guess I'll take it. Thanks.

Kids who are talked to in this way are more likely to become envious, narcissistic adults who need non-stop praise and affirmation to stave off depression and anxiety. Alternatives:

Parent: You can reach your goals if you put in the appropriate amount of time and effort.

Kid hears: I'm responsible for my achievements. I decide my place in society.

Parent: You're free to make your own mistakes. Learn from them.

Kid hears: There are consequences to every one of my actions and I'm responsible for them.

Parents: You need to work on that more if you want to get better.

Kid hears: I'm not that good, but I can get better.

First kid will think he's great and KNOWs he's not that good. Second kid thinks he sucks but KNOWS he can do better. Big difference. Beginning to see how someone as accomplished as Will Smith can act confident yet be so insecure? First kid will make excuses when he fails or only hang out with acolytes who praise him, feeding him bullshit bullshit bullshit so he grows up to rely on bullshit sandwiches (compliment followed by criticism followed by compliment) to get through work. Second kid will seek criticism, and screw the praise, that's a waste of time. There are standards to meet, visions to realize, and that's all that matters in life.

"I tried my best, I did and gave everything I could," parents tell me. No you did not. I was there, I saw it. I watched you fuck up your kid in your own fucked up way — the needless coddling, the glib praise, the undeserved gifts, the lame excuses, the anxious cheers. You're not a cheerleader, you're a parent, you're the coach. So parent and coach. Cheerleaders cheer, coaches teach and berate and motivate. Watch how the best coaches treat their players. Jim Calhoun, Bobby Knight, Jim Harbaugh: these motherfuckers scared the shit out of their kids and every single one of them is better for it. That's how you're supposed to treat your kids. That's how you win a championship.

Why is Self-Esteem Movement So Attractive?

It promises great results with little work. Takes effort to qualify a loaded statement like "you can be whatever you want." Takes even more effort to put such a statement in action: showing them what it takes, how it's done, by putting in the work yourself. Takes extraordinary effort to stay up with them through the night as they practice practice practice until your eyes are bloodshot and they get it right. Stop telling them how much you love them — that's a cop out — love requires ACTION, love is an act, not a feeling. Words are meaningless, people want acts of love, not bromides. No wonder glib slogans are more appealing. Allows parents to feign work and deflect blame when their kids turn into fuck ups.

The self-esteem movement promises Heaven on Earth. As with all attempts at making utopia happen on earth, the consequences are disastrous. Studies are showing: more violence, more depression, more envy, more anxiety, not less. Less achievement, less happiness, less self-confidence, less motivation, not more. Good news is that the Atlantic Monthly reading and NPR listening demographic has figured this out because their media sources have been telling them "reverse course reverse course we fucked up" for the past 10 years (see **Atlantic Monthly on Cult of Self-Esteem**). But how long will it take for the Cosmo and People mag reading demo to figure it out? Is it too late for them and their progeny, are they destined to a lifetime of bullshit sandwiches?

What Makes People Go Batshit Crazy?

People go crazy when their sense of self is at odds with other people's perceptions of themselves. Bridget thinks she's gorgeous. Because all her friends tell her so on Facebook. Mom and Dad too. Now lock her in a building full of Vogue cover models and make Anna Wintour (real-life Devil Meets Prada) her boss.

Let's see if she can last two months. She either emerges batshit crazy or a better person.

Put differently, dissonance between self-esteem and "reality" makes someone batshit crazy. That's why the person who thinks he's "oh so smart" avoids putting himself in situations that'll make him look stupid. Or the person who thinks she's funny and never notices that she's the only one laughing at her self-described "sarcastic wit" (whatever is being taught in English class, just stop stop stop it) will never have the courage to do stand-up on comedy night. People seek spaces and people who confirm their sense of self, their identity. And tend to avoid those who challenge their self-esteem. It's no wonder that those who invite and give criticism are the executives, while those who can't take it are managed staff, fed a steady diet of bullshit sandwiches to keep their fragile sense of self intact.

How to Treat a Model

Let's return to the model who dumps her boyfriend. Which response did you pick?

I think she dumped him because he complimented her looks too often. Guys, if you want to date a model, NEVER tell them how gorgeous they are. And not because she hears it all the time from those whose standards she disregards. Think about it, why did she become a model? Because she's tall and gorgeous? Plenty of women out there like that who don't become models, or try and fail. No, she became a model because she was insecure about her looks during her teen years. Perhaps schoolmates made fun of her lanky frame, hollowed cheeks, and buggy eyes. She grew accustomed to the criticism, desired it because it confirms her sense of reality, that she's not good looking. As she grew up and filled out and became what most consider beautiful, she stopped getting the criticism she desired. That's why she became a *successful* model, so some gay guy can pinch her thighs and tell her how fat and ugly she is, so she can be surrounded by people better than her. Her job confirms her reality. Her boyfriend didn't. So she dumped him and went to work.

Supermodels are supermodels because *they're never satisfied with their looks*, NOT because they think they're gorgeous.

When parents give their kids a reality — Heaven on Earth — that will never exist, they're giving pharma drug companies a few more customers. Kids can live their unreality for only so long before they're forced to accept that Santa doesn't exist; Lassie will die; Grandma is the tooth fairy; Grandpa watches barely legal porn; Mom's fucking her trainer; Dad sucked boyfriend's dick. That she's not as smart, pretty, and funny as she and her friends and family think she is. The ones prepared for reality will be able to change it. Those unprepared will be left confused, helpless, and crushed. That's reality.

CHAPTER 16 WHAT THE STORY OF ECHO AND NARCISSUS TELLS US ABOUT SELF-LOVE

I. What's worse, a hottie you can't have *who knows* he's a hottie? Or a hottie you can't have *who has no idea* she's a hottie? The former rejects you because he thinks he's too good for you. The latter because she thinks you're too good for her.

II. Did Narcissus know he's a hottie? All versions of the story I've read think he does, but I'm not so sure. Maybe he was just weirded out by all the attention he'd been receiving and wanted it to stop?

III. It's easy and comforting to feel superior to the hottie who knows she's a hottie. "Arrogant, superficial bitch, not worth the trouble," Larry the lackey tells himself before he runs home to jerk off to rape porn. No such option with the awkward hottie who has no idea he's gorgeous. Hating him is like hating a puppy you can't have.

IV. Find it improbable that Narcissus had never seen a reflection of himself until Nemesis, goddess of divine retribution, led him to do so so he'd fall in love with himself. Dude had to have been sipping water from streams and ponds all his life and nothing ever happened, never went on a selfie binge. It's more likely that Nemesis replaced his naivety (and nonchalance?) with vanity so when he got a drink at the pond, as he always does, he fell in love with himself and his selfie.

V. Nemesis doesn't get much action in the story. Yet she's more important than Echo, who is just a foil, and without Nemesis, there's no Narcissus. Nemesis doesn't just punish evil deeds, but also corrects undeserved good fortune, like making sure lazy Larry loses all 10 million of his lotto winnings within five, excruciating years. Born gorgeous? Don't think you're off the hook, and many fashion models would agree.

VI. My interpretation and re-telling of the story: Narcissus is a heart-breaker, not because he's vain, but because he's so not. Nemesis says this needs to stop, people — of dubious virtue — are wasting away because of him. She could turn him ugly, as gods and goddesses sometimes do as punishment, but that's not retributive *if Narcissus doesn't care if he's ugly* (my theory). Better to curse him with self-love instead, have him ogle his selfie until he dies. This way he learns what it's like for others to love him, to suffer as they have.

VII. The point is that Narcissus wasn't a narcissist until cursed by Nemesis. Narcissus recognizes the reflection as a selfie and his love of it as a disease. From Ovid's *Metamorphoses, Book III: 437-473:*

I am he. I sense it and I am not deceived by my own image. I am burn-

ing with love for myself. I move and bear the flames. What shall I do? Surely not court and be courted? Why court then? What I want I have. My riches make me poor. O I wish I could leave my own body! Strange prayer for a lover, I desire what I love to be distant from me. Now sadness takes away my strength, not much time is left for me to live, and I am cut off in the prime of youth. Nor is dying painful to me, laying down my sadness in death. I wish that him I love might live on, but now we shall die united, two in one spirit.

Narcissism, or vanity, kills Narcissus. And he knows it.

VIII. Takeaway: OUR nemesis — "the inescapable agent of someone's or something's downfall" — then, are those who tell us to love ourselves. And the moment we engage in self-love is when we begin to die as Narcissus had.

IX. "But self-love has nothing to do with narcissism," many object. What's self-love, then, according to promoters of self-love? Here's one definition I found online:

Self love *is the belief you hold that you are a valuable and worthy person.*

Valuable and worthy of what and to whom? According to every great religion and every great philosopher (yes, even Rousseau), everyone is a piece of shit, everyone deserves a life of pain and suffering and anyone who thinks otherwise is going batshit crazy. But let's play along and maintain the distinction between self-love and narcissism. How do you think narcissism begins? It begins with entitlement and that begins with thinking highly of oneself ("valuable" and "worthy," regardless of actions and results). Inches down this slope is selfishness, where one thinks one deserves *better* treatment than do others precisely because one is more "valuable" and "worthy," than are others. So it's looking like all signs point to "self-love" and its concomitant theories about "self-esteem" as the breeding ground of narcissism. That explains why Larry the loser can't figure out, while he's jerking off, why he doesn't bang the same hot babes as Sam the surgeon does. Or why mediocre Mina can't figure out why the man of her dreams doesn't propose to her and treat her like the beautiful and brilliant princess she thinks she is. Would this explain why everyone has the same complaint — narcissistic profiles — about online dating?

X. Self-love is the normalization of narcissism. That's why it's so dangerous, it's like having a disease without realizing it.

CHAPTER 17 WHY PEOPLE DON'T CHANGE

She's a White trash girl trying to escape her White trash world. At 21, she's got one foot out the door: 50k a year plus benefits as head manager of an independently owned retail store, where she's been working since 13. She saves enough to help her White trash family — grandma is especially proud of her, her siblings look up to her. She's saved enough to put 20 percent down on a modest house in a gentrifying not-quite-middle-class neighborhood. She has her shit together, a lot more so than those panicking college seniors who looked down on her but are now worried if they'll ever have a job that pays enough after graduation. Not bad for a high school drop out.

A customer — executive at a publicly traded company — is impressed with her work ethic, resourcefulness, and thoughtfulness. Hooks her up with a job as head manager of one of his struggling retail stores, where they've gone through three managers over the past year. He tells her she has the force of character to turn the store around, that she's a perfect fit. Compensation is 80k a year plus bonus plus vacation time and better bennies. Better career growth opportunities, potential for stock options, more sophisticated supply chain and IT infrastructure to work with, and those college educated bitches who made fun of her are now her bitches, making $12/hour. Fuck yeah.

She verbally commits, but can't sign when it's time, even though she's submitted her two weeks and reservations for going away party have been made by her colleagues. She ultimately stays put with the same business at the same position and lives out the rest of her not-quite-middle-class life in what quickly turns into an upper-middle class neighborhood, leaving her isolated and estranged from her surroundings.

What happened? What made White trash girl prefer the embarrassment of *not trying* over the *possible* embarrassment of failing?

(If you tell me it's low self-esteem, I'll graffiti your house with Hello Kitty stickers and paint your windows black).

"People Never Change, They Just Become More of Who They Really Are"

Marketing experts predicted that the recently promoted 28 year old woman buying the BMW was going to do so when she purchased her VW Jetta 5 years ago. Grandma didn't stop being a racist when she stopped using the N word sometime around 1974, she started watching her mouth because she's a chickenshit conformist. The only reason Johnny stopped doing anal 14 years ago is because his dick doesn't get hard enough for it anymore and he'd rather not think about that. The not-quite-middle-class teenager deleted all Facebook references to Jersey Shore only when she figured out that middle-class folks aren't supposed to admit to watching such shows, and not because she'd learned better taste and how to use her time more wisely.

Above examples illustrate the dictum, "people never change, they just become more of who they really are." Most changes are behavioral and not attitudinal (remember this distinction). Behavioral changes occur not because of fundamental change in a person's character, mindset, and sensibility, but because (pay attention, here comes the thesis) they're obligated and given the opportunity to change to *confirm their sense of self and reality*. Change, and the discipline and willpower that makes it possible, *is rooted in the act of regulating, sculpting, and imagining identity*. That's why peer pressure works and New Year's Resolutions don't.

Real change is change of mindset and attitude, not just behavior. Behavioral change alone is about maintaining status quo, it's about being fashionable, keeping up with the times instead of becoming a different person. Those who want to change their lives must change their mindset and attitude.

White Trash Girl Part II

White trash girl started working at 13 because she wanted things other kids had that she couldn't afford. She soon makes enough to become responsible for herself, buying not only her own toys, but also her own food and clothes. A few years later she makes enough to become responsible for her family, picking up some of the rent even after she stopped living with them. She becomes known as the responsible one, the caretaker, Santa to her siblings, the one who gets shit done — those archetypes combined became her *primary identity*. Her family and colleagues confirmed her identity.

One foot out the White trash door, why couldn't she get the other foot out and make a run for it? The opportunity was there. The scenarios if she takes the job:

* She fails at her new job, returns to her old job. Or a similar one making same as she did before. Back to the same old same old.

* She succeeds at her new job and eventually gets promoted to district manager, or is given a shot at corporate ladder.

Both of which seem a lot better than embarrassing herself to her colleagues and family by turning down a job she'd accepted. But she's playing on tilt, which is why she can't think straight, why she's emotional instead of rational. All she can think:

If I fail, that will be evidence that I'm not responsible and competent, and the world will reject me and I'll lose my identity as the responsible one, the caregiver, I'll be a loser again, they'll laugh at me again, everyone will make fun of me again...

At 13, she worked for toys. At 17, she worked to take care of herself. At 21, she worked to confirm her identity. She crumbled at the first perceived threat to her identity. Happens all the time. Check the socio-economic mobility data for non-immigrant Americans if you don't believe me.

What Makes People Batshit Crazy

Who is most likely to become batshit crazy? Pick:

a) White trash who knows she's White trash.

b) Middle-class who thinks she's high society

c) Rich kid slumming it with the hobos and peasants.

My picks: b, c, then a.

Who has the highest self-esteem? Pick:

a) White trash who knows she's White trash.

b) Middle-class who thinks she's high society

c) Rich kid slumming it with the hobos and peasants.

My picks: b, c, then a. What am I saying?

Being poor and having low self-esteem doesn't make one batshit crazy, but not knowing one's place does. White trash girl who knows she's White trash not only isn't batshit crazy, she isn't offensive because she's authentic, and that's why people want to help her, why we like her and root for her. Middle-class girl who thinks she's high society will never move up because she can only impress — with her contrived sensibilities — those who can't help her, and those who can either ignore her or gently laugh at her to put her in her place. Rich kid slumming is just a confused fuck trying to sort out feelings of guilt, pride, and ennui.

Dissonance between one's sense of self and "reality" is what makes one batshit crazy. That's why the middle-class girl who thinks she's high society avoids hanging out with rich kid slumming, who doesn't want to hang out with her anyway. She'll only hang out with those who confirm her sense of self, *her identity*. And that's precisely why she's not going anywhere except to therapy.

Self-Defense Mechanisms

You know, like rationalization. Projection. Denial. Google them.

The former high school beauty queen can't figure out why she isn't getting as much attention from guys (she's attracted to) as she used to even though she's gained 30 pounds since graduating from college 5 years ago. "Men around here are sissies, no courage to ask me out" she tells herself and her besties. Then she goes to a beauty salon and takes glamour photos of herself to post on Facebook. Since she's a nice girl and has a lot of friends, she gets the responses she needs to confirm her sense of self: 'like like like like like...' and comments like: "wow, this is like bringing a gun to a fist fight" from nice guy trying to convince the crowd that he is in fact a nice guy who therefore deserves some pussy; and the ubiquitous "you're so beautiful" from frenemy fishing for a similar compliment.

Self-defense mechanisms make us do some fucked up shit. Like purchase accessories, including houses, we can't afford. Like make bad business decisions that sink life savings. Like get a bullshit degree from a bullshit college, despite warnings about choosing the "wrong major" at the "wrong college." And then get another bullshit degree (Masters or JD) from yet another bullshit college when it turns out the first degree is useless. It's fucking madness but the madness continues because we filter out the information we don't want to hear and keep reading the articles that tell us we're right even when it's obvious to the Aliens watching us that we're not.

Ten young women on a trip in some faraway land are stopped and robbed. The robbers choose five to rape. What do you think the five not chosen are thinking and feeling? You think they're counting their blessings, "whew, at least I wasn't raped"? Or is NOT being picked to be raped WORSE than being raped?

(long pause)

That's how powerful self-defense of identity can be. That's why White trash girl turns irrational and quits life. The possibility that those who confirm her identity will stop doing so is too much for her to handle. She'd rather be miserable than risk losing her identity. Ironically, she ends up miserable AND loses her identity. The spark that made people want to help her is gone.

White trash girl was robbed the moment she was born. Fate wouldn't let her just be born poor, she had to be poor AND White, which is almost as bad as being Asian and the dumbest kid in school — there is no sympathy, there isn't even affirmative action, she's free game to be fucked with. When given a chance to grab the gun and shoot the dicks off the motherfuckers, she chose to do nothing. Did she do nothing because it wasn't worth the risk, or because she was hoping they'd pick her to be raped?

Choose a Reality That Will Make You Change

Cornell University study: **stupid people don't realize they're stupid. That's why they're stupid.** And the smartest don't realize they're that smart. Socrates said the same thing. Bill Gates said something similar: "Success is a lousy teacher. It makes smart people think they can't lose." Thanks for the confirmation, Cornell University.

Here's how it works: those who think they're "brilliant" or "not stupid" will rarely recognize their own stupidity. They will see and hear only that which confirms their identity. "Nah nah nah,

I didn't do that, I didn't say that, that can't be me, I'm not that dumb." Oh yes you are, we have the e-mail transcript to prove it, the evidence is there, you're in denial, you're purposely misreading it. Or we make excuses, blame others: "but it was raining, but it was busy, but the test was unfair, but the teacher is a racist, but but but but." Which are all short-term fixes that fuck up long-term goals. People grow and change only when there's failure failure failure AND the CAPACITY to learn from them. We stagnate when we avoid (the possibility of) failure, or worse, deny failure ever happened. Which is the same as denying our Original Sin, our total depravity, thus elevating ourselves to deity. One can do no wrong when one is god, right? So what happens when we have a room full of gods? You get Greek mythology: madness and batshit crazy. (see **How Cult of Self-Esteem Produces Fuck ups**).

Socrates again: it's easy to tell a person who thinks she's stupid that she's done something stupid. She's expecting to do something stupid, so she's looking for instances of her stupidity that will confirm her sense of self. Which is precisely why she grows and changes and moves up in her career, while Mr. Perfect blames reverse discrimination for not getting promoted. Once she masters a task, her sense of self demands she find a more difficult challenge, one where she fucks up and looks like a dumbass all over again.

Stupid, Useless, Cunt

If you really want to change — you're tired of banging your head on the same ceiling — choose a reality that will make you change into the person you want to be. "Manager didn't screw up on inventory, she was just testing to see if I'd catch the mistakes." "Girl who rejected me isn't racist, she simply found me obnoxious and repulsive." Test isn't biased, I just didn't study hard enough." "I'm late not because car battery died, but because I didn't change it before it died." "The CEO of Walmart isn't a lazy and greedy piece of shit who works 30 hours a week, he puts in 100 hour weeks and has done so his entire life." What I tell employees and those who ask me for advice on opening a restaurant:

You want reality? How's this for reality. For a month, make a three egg omelet every morning. Make it in less than a minute. If you can't make a perfect omelet in less than a minute, find a mirror. Now stare into your eyes and call yourself a "stupid, useless cunt." Three times. Because that's what someone is thinking every time you fuck up an order. And even if that isn't true, it NEEDS TO BE TRUE, YOU HAVE TO BELIEVE IT'S TRUE. If you don't, you'll fail, I guarantee it. "Stupid useless cunt" is what I call myself every morning. Makes my piss smell good, helps me piss straight. If you can't handle treating yourself this way, you're not going to last a month working here, much less running your own unbranded restaurant.

Choose the reality that'll make you the person you want to be, and not the reality that makes you feel good, short term. Choose life, not escape. Happy New Year, 2015!

ABOUT THE AUTHOR

Andrew An Ho

Author began cooking when he was 6 years old. He had his first samosa when he was 8. He experienced puberty at age 12. He didn't get kicked out of high school. He studied Socks, Drugs, and Rock and Roll in college; Semantics with Pedantics in grad school. Author is not an illegal alien. He may be a figment of your imagination. Some claim to have seen him. Others doubt his existence.

PRAISE FOR AUTHOR

"Rude. Rude rude rude...:

"He really is a Pig!"

"Quite possibly the worst call in experience in my entire life."

"Okay, so this place is completely insane. Sorry, Andrew, but you are batshit crazy."

"I'd give no star if I could. The Check in offer is rude & crude & just plain inappropriate for a business that deals with the public."

"Things can get dysfunctional at times..."

"I like going to Alive Juice Bar, despite the music, the sound of the blenders, and the frequency of customer ejections."

"...this was the most psychotic experience I've ever had."

"THE WORST PLACE EVER. He said he can't serve us because he doesn't like us!"

"It is true that the service is a tad bit abrasive, and takes getting used to just like the food."

"The owner is...not a lot of "warm & fuzzy..."

"...pretentious prick told me to go to Jamba Juice."

"This place is...super weird."

"I HATE this place so much my pussy hair is turning gray."

"It's infuriating to see these kind of things taking place."

"This place is an oasis from our decayed society – a safe haven for misanthropists so to speak."

"So... the owner claims to not serve assholes, but he was kinda acting like one behind the counter."

"Owner was telling new employee to call customers 'motherfucker'."

"This place isn't for everyone. I think that's their point."

"The awful owner told my son that the snowman will bite off his penis...he has nightmares now!"

"...this place is strange. I had a smoothie which was fine, but yea, the customer service is terrible."

"Although the juice is fine, among at least 5 different people that I interacted only one of them was actually nice. They rest were more like "Why are you here". Especially once I was about to leave because when I walked to the counter and gave them my order, nobody looked at my face and the guy (without making eye contact) said "Just yell it out and we'll make it ready" with a frustrated facial expression followed by a sigh."

"My review can't even begin to explain what a jerk this guy is – I can't believe anyone goes back.."

"I'm more mad I didn't get that monkey face middle finger thing."

- YELP REVIEWS OF ALIVE JUICE BAR

BOOKS IN THIS SERIES

Alive Juice Bar Series

How To Cook Like A Racist

This cookbook teaches you how to cook in the era of identity politics -- which meals you're allowed to cook, how to cook them, and whom you're allowed to serve. There's also a section on cooking for emotional eaters. There are Alive Juice Bar recipes throughout.

How To Go To School Like An Asian

The Juice Nazi is pissed, and you better believe there's a big difference between how those from Confucian cultures approach school and learning versus how your typical American does. This book includes lesson plans, education hacks, essays explaining how and why schools have and continue to fuck students up intellectually and emotionally, and a tutorial on how to go to school with an Asian mindset so you can learn faster and smarter.

How To Eat Like An Asshole

Do YOU eat like an asshole? How do you know if you eat like an asshole? Do you eat things that make you look like an asshole without realizing it? The Juice Nazi -- owner of Alive Juice Bar, located in a Seattle suburb -- mercilessly dissects American dining etiquette and American manners in general to reveal

cultural idiosyncrasies many don't notice. This book explains why what's typically considered as elegant and graceful, as good manners and fine taste, are actually signs of stupidity and depravity. This book will make those who consider themselves part of the American middle-class in manners and morals, squirm.

BOOKS BY THIS AUTHOR

I'm Not That Kind Of Girl: A Sadistic Basic Bitch Story

Roxanne G. is trying to get her boyfriend — Dummy Boy — to tattoo her name on his penis. He doesn't want to do that. So Roxanne uses her womanly wiles to train Dummy Boy to do what he doesn't want to do — go to a bookstore and hot yoga, eat sushi and dim sum, attend a symphony and bookreading…until he finally agrees to get the tattoo. She dumps him after he gets it, leaving him distraught and suicidal. Will Dummy Boy ever show his penis to another woman?

Made in the USA
Monee, IL
28 December 2020